FRANCIS DRAKE — ECHOES OF THE D...

TIMELINE

1492 – Columbus discovers the New World and claims it for Spain.

1494 – *Treaty of Tordesillas* divides the non-European world between Spain and Portugal.

1498 – Vasco da Gama opens a trade route to India for Portugal.

1517 – Martin Luther sparks the Protestant Reformation with his Ninety-Five Theses.

1522 – An expedition led by Ferdinand Magellan for Spain completes the first circumnavigation of the world.

1533 – Elizabeth Tudor is born.

1534 – Parliament passes the Act of Supremacy, making Henry VIII head of the Church of England.

1540 – Francis Drake is born.

1549 – The Drake family flees their farm in Devon for Chatham.

1552 – Francis Drake is fostered to the William Hawkins family of Plymouth to learn seafaring.

1553 – Mary Tudor becomes Queen and attempts to return England to Roman Catholicism.

1558 – Elizabeth I takes the throne and returns England to Protestantism.

1564 – Francis Drake sails with John Hawkins to the Caribbean.

1567 – Drake commands his first ship in a disastrous expedition to the Spanish Main led by John Hawkins.

1569 – Drake marries Mary Newman.

Francis Drake — Echoes of the Dragon's Drum

1572 – Drake leads raid on the Spanish Main, plundering a Spanish mule train of gold and silver in Panama.

1575 – Drake commands a ship in an English expedition to quell a rebellion in Ireland.

1580 – Drake is knighted by Elizabeth I after circumnavigating the globe.

1580 – Spain conquers Portugal after its king dies.

1581 – Mary Newman dies.

1585 – Drake marries his second wife, Elizabeth Sydenham.

1586 – Drake carries out raids in the West Indies.

1587 – Drake delays a Spanish invasion of England by raiding Cádiz.

1588 – The Spanish Armada is defeated.

1589 – Drake fails to capture Lisbon, then under the rule of Philip II of Spain.

1596 – Hawkins and Drake die in a final expedition against the Spanish in the Caribbean.

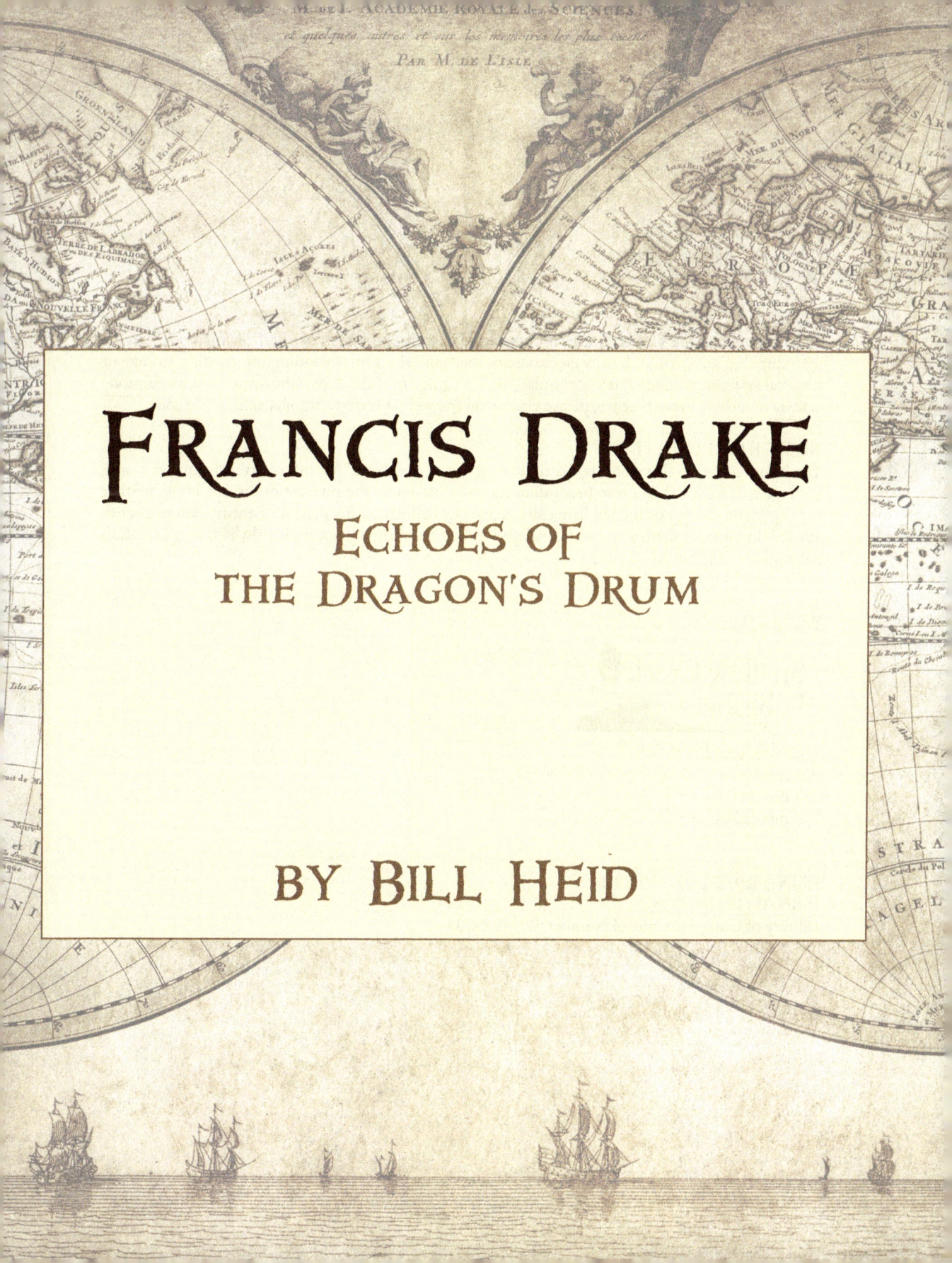

Francis Drake

Echoes of the Dragon's Drum

by Bill Heid

Francis Drake
Echoes of the Dragon's Drum
©2014 Bill Heid

NOTICE OF RIGHTS
Manufactured in the United States of America. All rights reserved. No part of this book may be reproduced in any form or by any electronic or mechanical means, including information storage or retrieval systems, without express permission in writing from the copyright owner. For more products by Solutions From Science, please visit us on the web at www.solutionsfromscience.com.

NOTICE OF LIABILITY
The information in this book is distributed on an "as is" basis, for informational purposes only, without warranty. While every precaution has been taken in the production of this book, neither the copyright owner nor the publisher shall have any liability to any person or entity with respect to any liability, loss, or damage caused or alleged to be caused directly or indirectly by the information contained in this book.

Published by:

Shallow Creek Publishers

Shallow Creek Publishers
An imprint of Heritage Press Publications, LLC
PO Box 561
Collinsville, MS 39325

ISBN-13: 978-1-937660-33-8
ISBN-10: 1937660338
Library of Congress Control Number: 2014949203

Table of Contents

Author's Notes 6

Prologue 8

Part I—A World Turned Upside Down 11

    Columbus, Magellan, and the Race for World Dominance 15

    Martin Luther, Henry VIII, and the Weakening Grip of Rome 18

Part II—From a Ship's Hulk to Captain of the Seas 23

    The Drakes Become People of the Sea 26

    Enter the Virgin Queen—Elizabeth I 30

    Drake's Introduction to Exploration with John Hawkins 35

    Privateer or Pirate 41

Part III—The Dragon Spreads His Wings 48

    Drake in the Spanish Main 51

    Rise to Importance Back Home 62

Part IV—Around the World and into National Legend 67

    Turning the Dream into Reality 70

    From England to South America 76

    Finishing the Course 90

Part V—Mortality Becomes Immortal 106

FRANCIS DRAKE ECHOES OF THE DRAGON'S DRUM

    Singeing King Philip's Beard 109

    Defeat of the Spanish Armada 120

    And with Imminent Danger Passed 128

    A Fitting Place to Die 131

Conclusion 135

John Stow, The Life And Death Of Sir Francis Drake 143

Disturb us, Lord, when
We are too well pleased with ourselves,
When our dreams have come true
Because we have dreamed too little,
When we arrived safely
Because we sailed too close to the shore.

Disturb us, Lord, when
With the abundance of things we possess,
We have lost our thirst
For the waters of life;
Having fallen in love with life,
We have ceased to dream of eternity
And in our efforts to build a new earth,
We have allowed our vision
Of the new Heaven to dim.

Disturb us, Lord, to dare more boldly,
To venture on wider seas
Where storms will show your mastery;
Where losing sight of land,
We shall find the stars.
We ask you to push back
The horizon of our hopes;
And to push us into the future
In strength, courage, hope, and love.

—most historians attribute this prayer to Sir Francis Drake

Mʀˢ DE L'ACADEMIE ROYALE des SCIENCES
et quelques autres et sur les memoires les plus recens
PAR M. DE L'ISLE

FRANCIS DRAKE — ECHOES OF THE DRAGON'S DRUM

Author's Notes

This work is not primarily a history. History is the chronological account of an era while a biography focuses on one man within that time. As such, a good biography seeks to answer the question, "What made this man significant for his time and continues to make him significant for the times that follow?" History sets people, places, events, and dates in a broad panorama. Biography examines one man's pilgrimage through this world. As Sir Edmund Gosse has phrased it, biography is "the faithful portrait of a soul in its adventures through life."

There are many fine works that cover the history of the 16th century and provide a bigger picture of the era, and I encourage you to read them. Michael Turner of The Drake Exploration Society has written several accounts of Drake's explorations that follow Drake on every adventure in painstaking detail. Turner has spent years following the paths of the *Golden Hind* and Drake's other ships to compile what amounts to a modern day travelogue and should be commended for a job well done. Comprehensive biographies that offer a more detailed history include the works of John Cummins, John Sugden, Charles River, and William Wood. Sugden's work is the best researched and fairly balanced biography of all.

Francis Drake: Echoes of the Dragon's Drum is neither scholarly history nor exhaustive biography. Instead, it seeks to provide an accurate and entertaining biographical sketch that will encourage you to learn more about the man. In every man's life there are defining moments—events

FRANCIS DRAKE — ECHOES OF THE DRAGON'S DRUM

that set the course of his future, the lasting impression left by this man or that woman, and a whole range of intangibles that can only be called Providence. This work focuses on those moments that defined the man Francis Drake.

With this said, we cannot ignore the history surrounding Drake. In the preface to his monumental four volume biography of Winston Churchill, William Manchester observes: "There can be no enlightening life which does not include an account of the man's times. This need for context is even greater when the central figure is a towering statesman. It is impossible to understand Churchill and his adversaries in the 1930s, for example, without grasping the British revulsion against the horrors of World War I.[1]" No man is born or exists in a vacuum, and what fills that space is where history and biography intersect.

Henry Ford, father of the modern automobile era, was quoted in a 1916 edition of the Chicago Tribune as saying, "History is more or less bunk. It's tradition. We don't want tradition. We want to live in the present, and the only history that is worth a tinker's damn is the history that we make today."[2] In spite of his monumental achievements, Ford failed to understand that the history he was making would have ongoing consequences. It is still directly affecting the history being made today. Ford failed to see his place in history was part of a bigger whole.

Whether Francis Drake fully understood his place in history is doubtful. He was much too busy living his life to be caught up in ensuring that his legacy would endure. Even after circumnavigating the globe, becoming

Francis Drake — Echoes of the Dragon's Drum

mayor of Plymouth, and being knighted by the Queen, Drake found that the sea always beckoned him to her. He did write down some of his adventures, but never produced an extensive memoir. He left such things to those who came after him. Hopefully, this work will add a few more brush strokes to the portrait of a life that deserves to be remembered.

FRANCIS DRAKE — ECHOES OF THE DRAGON'S DRUM

PROLOGUE

Who was Francis Drake? His contemporaries could have given many answers. He was a national hero, a rogue, a privateer in the Queen's command, a scurrilous pirate pillaging innocent Spanish outposts. He was an arrogant and insolent sea-urchin, who didn't know his place. He was a faithful Protestant, committed to Christ. Or he was the bane of the one true Church. To Roman Catholic Spain, Drake was a dragon who consumed their precious treasure ships. But for the English, the wind from that dragon's wings empowered their island nation to become a global empire.

The custom of translating books and maps into Latin led to Drake's first association with dragons. Engraver Theodore de Bry Latinized his name to Franciscus Draco ("Francis the Dragon"). Dragons held a special place in the folklore of his world. They could be either a protector or a fearful adversary, and which dragon Drake was is subject to the source consulted. But one thing is certain: Drake was a game-changer in the course of the Western world. Deprived of lordships and the monikers of those born to wealth and influence, El Draco was a title he alone earned. Queen Elizabeth would knight him Sir Francis, but only his exploits, character, daring, and what some called luck and others knew as Providence, would make him the legend he came to be.

A part of the challenge of writing a biography of a man who has become legend is sorting through fact and fiction. How does one know the absolute truth about anyone who died over 400 years ago, especially when there are so many seemingly credible yet divergent accounts?

FRANCIS DRAKE   ECHOES OF THE DRAGON'S DRUM

Consider the following two stories from Drake's voyage beyond the Straights of Magellan and across the Pacific. Is one fact and the other fiction? Or is there something of a mixture of the two that makes men like Francis Drake so interesting to consider?

In his forthcoming book, *Francis Drake in Nova Albion—The Mystery Restored*, Oliver Seeler tells of an incident that occurred around Christmas of 1579 when Drake and his crew entered the water of what we now call the Indonesian Archipelago. Two years of their famous voyage were behind them, the ship was loaded with plunder, and now Drake was intent on capping his expedition with new English influence in the territory and with a few tons of the region's much sought after spices.

Landfall among friendly locals included negotiations for much needed items to reprovision the ship for the long trek across the Indian Ocean. Drake came to meet Babu, king of the island of Teranate. The king's court and brightly colored accessories are described in vivid detail by a contemporary in *The World Encompassed by Sir Francis Drake* (1628). During that meeting, the king had his servants deliver a special provision to Drake's ship.

> "Accordingly ... we received what was there to be had ... an imperfect liquid sugar, a fruit ... cocoes ... and a kind of meal ... ; whereof they make a kinde of cake which will keepe good at least 10 years; of this last we made the greatest quantity of our provision ..."[3]

Not long after Drake departed Teranate, he found an uninhabited island where the *Golden Hind* stayed for 26 days while the crew made repairs

FRANCIS DRAKE   ECHOES OF THE DRAGON'S DRUM

and collected an abundance of foods necessary to prevent scurvy. With such fresh stores now available, King Babu's "fruitcakes" were set aside and forgotten in the recesses of the ship's hold. When the *Golden Hind* arrived back in England, the crew unloaded those cakes and found they looked more like ballast stones than anything edible. Drake's men asked what they should do with the heavy cakes. Drake ordered them given out freely to the local townsfolk.

How could Drake have known, asks Seeler, that he had started a Christmas tradition that would persist to this day? Had the seaman passed on a gift, a cake, that is somewhat edible and has a shelf life like no other dessert?

The next snippet of Drake legend comes from the same voyage. Distrust and sometimes outright disdain was common between the sailors, who were commoners, and the "gentlemen" who often financed and accompanied their investment. Tension between the classes was common, but was usually kept in check by Drake's kind, yet ironhanded leadership and by a mutual desire for a successful voyage. But things unraveled a bit when Drake became convinced that Thomas Doughty, an aristocrat and former commander of the flagship *Pelican*, had become a greater liability than the expedition could afford. Before all was said and done, Doughty was accused not only of sedition, but witchcraft. Standing on the same barren place where, 50 years earlier, Magellan had executed and dismembered a mutinous crewman, Francis Drake ordered Doughty's execution.

What happened once the sentence was pronounced is hard for anyone in this age to comprehend. In his *Rounding the Horn* (2005), Dallas Murphy writes: "That night, as if actors in a grand Elizabethan drama, Drake and Doughty first received communion . . . and '. . . after this holy repast they dined, also at the same table, together, as cheerful in sobriety, as ever in their lives they had done aforetime: each cheering up the other . . . as if some journey only had been at hand.' And then the executioner showed up. Doughty was led to a corner of the island and beheaded. I admit I do not understand the Doughty story, but there it was. . . ."

The story of the odd affair of executioner and condemned taking communion and enjoying a meal together before the latter was relieved of his head is, in fact, confirmed by numerous contemporary sources. Oliver Seeler, however, is quick to admit the story of King Babu and his fruitcakes is for the most part, "creative speculation."

Victor Hugo said, "History has its truth, and so has legend. Legendary truth is of another nature than historical truth. Legendary truth is invention whose result is reality. Furthermore, history and legend have the same goal; to depict eternal man beneath momentary man."[4] Part of the purpose of this biography is to sort through the fact and fiction of Francis Drake's life. To do so requires listening to the words of those who dealt with him directly and considering the man as something bigger than the separate incidents that made up his life.

My aim is to neither extol nor denigrate Francis Drake. Rather, it is to consider what made this man something more than the historical

FRANCIS DRAKE — ECHOES OF THE DRAGON'S DRUM

fragments depicted by biographers and poets. It is, as Hugo said, to find the eternal man behind the momentary man.

One of the legends that has persisted across centuries concerns the drum Drake carried with him on his voyages. It is said that whenever England finds herself in perilous times, she will hear the beating of the drum as encouragement to persevere. This is not just the idle talk of old men in pubs; the legend has been referenced by the likes of Lord Nelson and Margaret Thatcher. Even now, some claim they can hear echoes of the Dragon's drum.

Mre DE L'ACADEMIE ROYALE des SCIENCES
et quelques autres et sur les memoires les plus recens
PAR M. DE L'ISLE

Part I
A World Turned Upside Down

Mᴿˢ DE L'ACADEMIE ROYALE des SCIENCES
et quelques autres et sur les memoires les plus recens
PAR M. DE L'ISLE

FRANCIS DRAKE — ECHOES OF THE DRAGON'S DRUM

Listen to me and you shall hear, news hath not been this thousand year:
Since Herod, Caesar, and many more, you never heard the like before.
Holy-dayes are despis'd, new fashions are devis'd.
Old Christmas is kicked out of Town
Yet let's be content, and the times lament,
You see the world turn'd upside down.

—English Ballad

Today Sir Francis Drake is generally out of favor with historians. They find him politically incorrect. They make the mistake of judging a man from the 16th century by 21st century standards with no consideration for the world into which he was born. In his review of Harry Kelsey's biography of Drake, N.A.M. Roger notes exactly this weakness. Roger writes that Kelsey's "focus is exceedingly close: anything that cannot be seen through a microscope is not seen at all. There is nothing to explain the political and social situation of 16th-century England, nothing on the international and diplomatic context that generated the English-Spanish war, nothing on the development of shipbuilding, navigation, naval tactics and strategy. The result is that Drake is implicitly judged not against his standards but ours."[5]

This kind of historical deconstruction is quite in vogue these days, but does a great disservice to those seeking to understand and learn

FRANCIS DRAKE — ECHOES OF THE DRAGON'S DRUM

from a figure like Francis Drake. When one takes Kelsey's approach, the result is a straw man to which one can attach a multitude of sins while failing to take into account how the real man measured up against the standards of his day.

Francis Drake was not born in a vacuum, and because of that, it is essential that we take time to educate ourselves on the world into which Drake was born. To do otherwise is to end up with a biography like Kelsey's that views his subject as though his ideas and actions were somehow unique. Worse yet, such a narrow view fails to see the bigger picture which

Portrait of Sir Francis Drake by Crispin de Passe, 1598.

FRANCIS DRAKE   ECHOES OF THE DRAGON'S DRUM

reveals Francis Drake as a man who rose above most of those around him.

Roger is correct when he observes: "It is useless to write Drake off as a leader with a paranoid suspicion of disloyalty without describing the situation of a commander of humble origins in an age when all authority was based on birth, and he had gentlemen serving under him who had every reason to expect to be in charge. It is easy enough to find 16th-century witnesses who attacked Drake, for he had many personal enemies and professional rivals. What the modern reader needs to know is why he was attacked, and to what extent we believe his enemies. To answer that, an author has to take his eye away from the microscope and look around."[6]

Because Drake played such a key role in the world events of his day and because he was more or less a national hero, there are a wealth of first-hand accounts of interactions with other people. True, the English and Spanish versions of Drake are quite different. But if you hear what these people had to say about him, understand why they thought as they did, and weigh all that in consideration of the times, it is possible to come up with an honest portrait of what made Francis Drake legendary.

The Protestant Reformation is one of a series of events that set off a seismic shift in the social, political, and religious world into which Francis Drake was born. The fifty years that led up to Drake's birth saw one presupposition after another fall. The half-century from Christopher Columbus's discovery of the West Indies to Henry VIII's decision to remove the English church from papal control was marked by nothing

FRANCIS DRAKE   ECHOES OF THE DRAGON'S DRUM

but surprises. To borrow from Bob Dylan, "The Times They Were a Changin'."

From common sailor to exalted Lord, everyone was trying to figure out how he fit into the new paradigm of a world seen through much bigger lenses than ever before. More often than not, all that change eventually settled back into comfortable norms: Lords were Lords, and commoners were commoners. The state a man was born into was where he could count on remaining. But not Francis Drake! As a young man, he looked out upon the seas and determined to take advantage of what lay beyond the horizon. He would grab those cataclysmic changes by the nape of the neck and ride them where Providence led.

FRANCIS DRAKE — ECHOES OF THE DRAGON'S DRUM

COLUMBUS, MAGELLAN, AND THE RACE FOR WORLD DOMINANCE

Whoopie ti-yi-yo
Farewell, Magellan
You almost made it
It's really not fair
Whoopie ti-yi-yo
Oh, ghost of Magellan
The East Indies islands
Were right over there!

—Paul Rugg and John P. McCann

Drake's era of change began in 1492 when Christopher Columbus sailed across the Atlantic with the odd notion that one could sail westward and end up in India. By his calculations, the distance from the Azores to the spice-rich East was about three thousand miles and therefore within the reach of the small vessels of his day. For years the courts of Portugal and Spain endured his perpetual insistence that all he needed was their royal backing to prove his calculations correct. The cost of such an endeavor was so expensive that no individual, no matter how wealthy, could finance such an attempt. Everything was dependent on royal approval and money.

FRANCIS DRAKE ⛵ ECHOES OF THE DRAGON'S DRUM

Painting by Circle of Joachim Patinir circa 1540 - Portuguese carracks off a rocky coast.

Eventually, the king and queen of Spain, fresh from expelling the last of the Moors from Iberia, consented to finance three vessels for Columbus. This investment constituted a major gamble for the war-stressed treasury of Spain, but if Columbus succeeded, that treasury would rapidly fill with the proceeds of trade. Columbus's mathematical calculations were off by quite a bit, but the land he found, soon to be called the West Indies, opened a gateway to treasures far greater than the spices of China and India. And though Columbus, until his dying breath, clung to his belief that he had discovered islands not far from India, the king and queen of Spain quickly realized they had found a new source of much needed capital in the form of gold and silver. They realized, too, that the vast treasure was guarded by a local population hardly equipped to fend off the weapons of their soldiers.

FRANCIS DRAKE   ECHOES OF THE DRAGON'S DRUM

Speaking of this era, William Wood notes: "The leading pioneers in the Age of Discovery were sons of Italy, Spain, and Portugal. Cabot... was an Italian, though he sailed for the English Crown and had an English crew. Columbus, too, was an Italian, though in the service of the Spanish Crown. It was the Portuguese Vasco da Gama who in the very year of John Cabot's second voyage (1498) found the great sea route to India by way of the Cape of Good Hope. Two years later the Cortereals, also Portuguese, began exploring the coasts of America as far northwest as Labrador. Twenty years later... the Portuguese Magellan, sailing for the King of Spain, discovered the strait still known by his name, passed through it into the Pacific, and reached the Philippines.... In 1513, the Spaniard Balboa had crossed the Isthmus of Panama and waded into the Pacific, sword in hand, to claim it for his king. Then came the Spanish explorers—Ponce de Leon, De Soto, Coronado, and many more—and later on the conquerors and founders of New Spain—Cortes, Pizarro, and their successors."[7]

Up to this point, the half-century of world changing events hinged on the patronage of Italy, Spain, and Portugal. Europe, entangled in what amounted to family and religious feuds, was hungry for new sources of revenue, and the treasures of the New World were too alluring to ignore. Spain and its tiny seafaring neighbor Portugal commanded the largest fleets in Europe and were so far ahead in the game of global exploration that other players such as England seemed hardly of consequence. As a result Portugal and Spain were in danger of seeing their disputes over "discovered" lands escalate into a costly war that papal Rome was determined to circumvent.

FRANCIS DRAKE ECHOES OF THE DRAGON'S DRUM

So Pope Alexander VI issued the bull *Inter Caetera*, which established a line of demarcation between Portugal's African and Asian sphere of influence and Spain's New World. The lines established by the Pope favored Spain, which was, as Dudley writes, "unsurprising, considering that Pope Alexander VI was born in Spain."[8] Displeased with the arrangement, Portugal bypassed the Pope and sought direct negotiations with Spain. These resulted in the Treaty of Tordesillas in 1494.

Seafaring of that day was not an exact science. Often times the winds played more into geo-political affairs than anything else, and such was the case with the treaty. A Portuguese captain, blown far off course, accidentally discovered South America in 1500; this is the reason the people of Brazil speak Portuguese to this day. Twenty-three years later, Magellan's expedition completed the first circumnavigation of the world. Along the way, it claimed for Spain Portuguese islands in the East Indies, and the Spanish crown suddenly concluded that the Tordesillas line extended completely around the globe. Tiny Portugal was soon overwhelmed by the rapid growth of an empire that lacked the population or resources of neighboring Spain. It was only a matter of time before her aspirations of world domination ended. In 1580 Portugal became a Spanish province.

The bull that divided the world in half gave the pope's tacit blessing to Spanish and Portuguese exploration and colonization. As a result the two were free to divide the spoils as long as Rome could claim all the souls and its fair share of the treasure.

England, however, was an "ill-defined amoebic shape squeezed, like an afterthought of the mapmakers, into the northwest periphery" of the world map, "far from the Mediterranean center of the civilized world."[9] And within the decade, her geopolitical position dramatically declined. She was left out and behind when it came both to trade and the treasures that always accompanied exploration. With no new trade routes in sight, England had little hope of developing her commercial interests.

M. de l'Academie Royale des Sciences
et quelques autres et sur les memoires les plus recens
Par M. de L'Isle

FRANCIS DRAKE — Echoes of the Dragon's Drum

Martin Luther, Henry VIII, and the Weakening Grip of Rome

If God had not been on our side
And had not come to aid us,
The foes with all their power and pride
Would surely have dismayed us;
For we, His flock, would have to fear
The threat of men both far and near
Who rise in might against us.

Their furious wrath, did God permit,
Would surely have consumed us
And as a deep and yawning pit
With life and limb entombed us.
Like men o'er whom dark waters roll
Their wrath would have engulfed our soul
And, like a flood, o'erwhelmed us.

Blest be the Lord, who foiled their threat
That they could not devour us;
Our souls, like birds, escaped their net,
They could not overpower us.
The snare is broken—we are free!
Our help is ever, Lord, in Thee,
Who madest earth and Heaven.

—Martin Luther

FRANCIS DRAKE — ECHOES OF THE DRAGON'S DRUM

With Spain virtually controlling the sea routes to the Caribbean, or as it came to be called, "the Spanish Main," King Henry VII (1485-1509) of England made a major contribution to Anglo-American history. On March 5, 1496, just four years after Columbus's first voyage, Henry granted a patent to John Cabot and his three sons to pursue colonization in the Americas. True, Cabot was Italian, but his efforts would be under the flag of England. The charter given to the Cabots reads:

Henrie, by the grace of God, King of England and France, and Lord of Irelande, to all, to whom these presentes shall come, Greeting—Be it knowen, that We have given and granted, and by these presentes do give and grant for Us and Our Heyres, to our well beloved John Gabote, citizen of Venice, to Lewes, Sebastian, and Santius, sonnes of the sayde John, and to the heires of them and every of them, and their deputies, full and free authoritie, leave, and Power, to sayle to all Partes, Countreys, and Seas, of the East, of the West, and of the North, under our banners and ensignes, with five shippes, of what burden or quantitie soever they bee: and as many mariners or men as they will have with them in the saide shippes, upon their owne proper costes and charges, to seeke out, discover, and finde, whatsoever Iles, Countreyes, Regions, or Provinces, of the Heathennes and Infidelles, whatsoever they bee, and in what part of the worlde soever they bee, whiche before this time have been unknowen to all Christians. We have granted to them also, and to every of them, the heires of them, and every of them, and their deputies, and have given them licence to set up Our banners and ensignes in every village, towne, castel, yle, or maine lande, of them newly founde. And that the aforesaide John and his sonnes, or

FRANCIS DRAKE   ECHOES OF THE DRAGON'S DRUM

their heires and assignes, may subdue, occupie, and possesse, all such townes, cities, castels, and yles, of them founde, which they can subdue, occupie, and possesse, as our vassailes and lieutenantes, getting unto Us the rule, title, and jurisdiction of the same villages, townes, castels, and firme lande so founde.[10]

Finally, England had a foothold in the New World.

At this time, England and Spain were rivals in trade, but not in religion; like Spain, Portugal, and Italy, England was still loyal to papal Rome. But the actions of Martin Luther and Henry VIII would change everything and set the stage for the career of Francis Drake. What began as a race for treasure and trade was about to become a struggle between Rome and the English Reformation. That struggle would prove to be a major factor in Drake's tenacity and success.

On All Hallow's Eve in 1517, less than six years before Magellan began his famous voyage, a German monk named Martin Luther nailed a set of papers to the church door in Wittenberg and shook the Roman Catholic world to its very foundations. His *Ninety-Five Theses,* aimed at the abuse of indulgences, unleashed a maelstrom of religious controversy upon Europe. Luther never intended to rebel against the church or leave it, but in questioning the sale of indulgences, he questioned the authority of the pope and the relationship of grace to works in man's salvation. Eventually, Luther came to understand that the Bible teaches justification by faith alone—that man is made right with God, not by his own works, but through faith in Christ and His finished work on the cross.

FRANCIS DRAKE — ECHOES OF THE DRAGON'S DRUM

Luther found himself at odds with the pope's best debaters. But Luther proved the more competent as he stoutly defended justification by faith and attacked the crass materialism that infected the church. The result of Luther's ministry was a biblical reformation, a re-shaping, of much of the German church in terms of Scripture.

At the same time other godly pastors and theologians all over Europe were discovering and preaching the same truths in their own countries. These men were called Reformers and Protestants.

Their work, the Protestant Reformation, spread like wildfire across Europe. Spain, however, remained firmly in the Roman fold.

When Henry VIII ascended the throne in 1509, however, his concern was hardly religious. But he was concerned with control of the English Channel, or as he called it, the "Broade Ditch." His commitment to England's naval power continued to his last act as king when he established the Office of the Admiralty and Marine Affairs in 1546. King Henry's leadership transformed England's navy from an ancient to a modern fleet.

Throughout his reign, Henry took a personal delight and interest in everything to do with ships and shipping. Though given to deteriorating health and temperament in the latter years of his reign, he still mixed freely with naval men and merchant skippers, visited the dockyards, sponsored several improved types of vessels, and thoroughly mastered scientific gunnery. This interest in all things naval could not have come at a more important time for an England about to fall out of favor with papal Rome.

FRANCIS DRAKE   ECHOES OF THE DRAGON'S DRUM

Henry wanted a male heir. He knew from England's recent history (the War of the Roses) that civil war would likely erupt if there were no clear heir to the throne. When his Spanish wife Catherine didn't produce a son, Henry looked elsewhere. He found a young Anne Boleyn and wanted an annulment of his marriage to Catherine. The pope refused to grant it. Henry pushed a series of acts through Parliament that made him temporal head of the Church of England. Henry got his annulment from his own archbishop. Religious reform followed slowly in the wake of these external changes.

Henry's break with Rome created his nation's greatest challenge, and his support of a modern navy offered its best hope of salvation. England's chief rivals were led by the two greatest monarchs of continental Europe, Francis I of France and Charles V of Spain. Henry, Francis, and Charles were all young, doggedly ambitious, and exceptionally capable men. Charles ruled vast dominions scattered over both the New World and the Old. The destiny of much of the world rested mostly on the rivalry between these three and their successors. The ships and seaman they commanded would make all the difference.

Up to this point, ships were little more than floating castles designed to carry armies to their next point of attack. According to Wood, Henry VIII "was the first of national leaders to grasp the full significance of what could be done by broadsides fired from sailing ships against the mediaeval type of vessel that still depended more on oars than on sails."[11] He proved to be more than a detached ruler when it came to his navy; he was a patron of the sea. His friendship with a shipwright led to immediate acceptance of a technique that became a game-changer

FRANCIS DRAKE   ECHOES OF THE DRAGON'S DRUM

in the balance of power both in Europe and ultimately the rest of the world. A year or so before the birth of Francis Drake, Fletcher of Rye discovered the art of tacking. Wood explains how this simple yet dramatic method of sailing changed everything: "Never before had any kind of craft been sailed a single foot against the wind ... But now Fletcher ran out his epoch-making vessel, with sails trimmed fore and aft, and dumbfounded all the shipping in the Channel by beating his way to windward against a good stiff breeze. This achievement marked the dawn of the modern sailing age."[12] Long stymied by the prevailing winds that blew northward, England's ships could now sail directly against those winds to face any oncoming enemies from the south.

And so it happened in 1545 that Henry, with a new-born modern fleet, was able to turn defiantly on his neighbor across the Channel. His lifelong interest in ships and those who made them paid off on an oceanic scale. There was no great sea battle during the reign of Henry VIII, but he was able to send out squadron upon squadron of ships to harass the shipbuilding yards of those planning to attack England. The conversion from a floating army to a real naval fleet—from galleys moved by oars to ships moved by sails—was a monumental change. The English no longer had to board enemy ships; they could broadside them instead. England was first in developing the only kind of navy that would count in any struggle for oversea dominion. With the discovery of the Americas and the treasure that lay there, sea power was no longer a question of coasts and landlocked waters, but of all the outer oceans of the world.

The decade that saw the invention of tacking and thus the birth of

FRANCIS DRAKE — ECHOES OF THE DRAGON'S DRUM

the first modern naval fleet set the stage for all that was to come. The 1540s was a crucial decade for England in other ways. Protestantism took firmer root with the new Prayer Book issued by Henry's successor, Edward VI. News of the gold mines of the New World reached the Old. And birth cries announced the arrival of Francis Drake.

ACADEMIE ROYALE des SCIENCES
et quelques autres et sur les memoires les plus recens
PAR M. DE L'ISLE
GROENLAND
B. DE BAFFIN
BAYE D'HUDSON
CANADA
MEXIQUE
GOLFE DE MEXIQUE
Guatimala
Isles Gualagoas
Detroit de Magellan
Antarctique
MER GLACIALE
TERRES
DU NORD

Part II

From a Ship's Hulk to Captain of the Seas

PART II

FROM A SHIPS
HELM TO CAPTAIN
OF THE SEAS

FRANCIS DRAKE ECHOES OF THE DRAGON'S DRUM

*And now let us see how a dwarf,
standing on the mount of God's providence,
may prove an overmatch for a giant.*

—William Fuller, *The Holy State*

Not long after the famous rout of the Spanish Armada by England, Pope Sixtus V voiced what many came to ask during the life of Francis Drake: who is this man? Listen as Sixtus wrings his hands in frustration over this upstart from Plymouth:

> *"Just look at Drake! Who is he? What forces had he? And yet he burned twenty-five of the King's ships at Gibraltar, and as many again at Lisbon; he has robbed the flotilla, and sacked San Domingo. His reputation is so great that his countrymen flock to him to share his booty. We are sorry to say it, but we have a poor opinion of this Spanish Armada, and fear some disaster."*[13]

Sir Francis Drake by Marcus Gheeraerts.

But it wasn't just the Spanish who were perplexed by Francis Drake.

FRANCIS DRAKE — ECHOES OF THE DRAGON'S DRUM

When later in his life, Drake was granted a favored place in Queen Elizabeth's inner circle, he became painfully aware that he was still an outsider looking in, a commoner interloping on the domain of gentry and wealth. He would always be reminded that he had been born into a society that idolized status and birth.

Drake is not the only war dog who experienced difficulty fitting in with the powers-that-be once the fog of war cleared. Whether it was Churchill or Thatcher or Drake, all had one thing in common: warriors are doers first and diplomats second. However, a man of Drake's background rising to national and international prominence was far less likely in 16th century England than in any time since.

Yet just a few years after becoming captain of his first ship, Drake was the talk of the nation. Even before his death, there was a wealth of poetry, sonnets, and songs extolling his exploits. Less than a century later came an opera dramatizing the life of England's now favorite son. And while the names of most of England's aristocrats are long forgotten, there remain numerous biographies, publications, historical societies, and streets and boulevards that remind us of a man who transcended his humble beginnings.

To answer Pope Sixtus's question as to who Francis Drake really was, we should begin with his family and the factors that caused the Drakes to abandon their farm and become people of the sea.

The Drakes Become People of the Sea (1540-1555)

They love the sea,
Men who ride on it
And know they will die
Under the salt of it

Let only the young come,
Says the sea.

Let them kiss my face
And hear me.
I am the last word
And I tell
Where storms and stars come from.

—Carl Sandburg

A few contemporary accounts, both English and Spanish, refer to Francis Drake's father as a sailor, but legal documents of 1548 indicate that he made his living off the land. In particular, he is listed as a shearman, one who shears cloth. All told, Edmund Drake and his wife Mary had twelve sons of whom Francis was the oldest. They were by all accounts a family of modest means, though Francis Russell, the Earl of Bedford, did offer his first name to the eldest son. He was his godfather.

FRANCIS DRAKE ECHOES OF THE DRAGON'S DRUM

It was a time of dramatic religious shifts as England was first loyal to Rome, then mildly Protestant under Henry VIII, more staunchly Protestant under Edward VI, Roman Catholic under Queen Mary, and then Protestant again under Elizabeth I. As a result, some parts of England leaned more toward Rome, others more toward the Reformation.

Sir Francis Drake's House near Severn Bridge, Gatcombe, England. Courtesy of Snapshots of the Past, Wikimedia Commons.

The town of Francis Drake's birth was not a good place for those adamantly Protestant. When the Drakes sided with the new version of the Prayer Book endorsed by the Crown, they soon found themselves forced to move to Kent where most Protestants agreed with their views.

Edmund proved so enthusiastic for the Protestant faith that he was first made a deacon in the local church and then assigned the pastorate of Upnor Church. Eventually, the elder Drake was made a chaplain in the Royal Navy. As biographer William Wood so colorfully describes it, "[Edmund's] friends at court then made him a sort of naval chaplain to the men who took care of His Majesty's ships laid up in Gillingham Reach on the River Medway, just below where Chatham Dockyard stands to-day. Here, in a vessel too old for service,

FRANCIS DRAKE — ECHOES OF THE DRAGON'S DRUM

most of Drake's eleven brothers were born to a life as nearly amphibious as the life of any boy could be. The tide runs in with a rush from the sea at Sheerness, only ten miles away; and so, among the creeks and marshes, points and bends, through tortuous channels and hurrying waters lashed by the keen east wind of England, Drake reveled in the kind of playground that a sea-dog's son should have."[14]

Raising twelve boys in Kent was no easy feat for the Drakes, and prospects for advancement were practically nil. So Edmund found an apprenticeship for Francis with the captain of a barque. These little boats used for transporting goods across the English Channel proved to be excellent training for Drake years later when he took advantage of his lighter, faster ships in the shallow Caribbean waters of the Spanish Main. In spite of being just ten years old, Francis grew quite adept at manning his barque to the point that a contemporary wrote that the boy "so pleased the old man by his industry that, being a bachelor, at his death he bequeathed his bark unto him by will and testament."[15] This early training on the sea moved Drake to leave the confines of English waters in his early 20s to sail with his cousin, John Hawkins.

To understand Drake's character and style of command, we must understand something of English social structure during that era. The class structure of Elizabethan England had the flexibility of a ship's main mast; a man's station of life at birth generally persisted until death. Rules for how to address anyone of title were precise and strict. For example, Francis Russell, Drake's godfather, was the Earl of Bedford. Protocol dictated that he be addressed as Lord Bedford, but never Lord Russell or Lord Francis. This class structure was well-defined and

FRANCIS DRAKE — ECHOES OF THE DRAGON'S DRUM

generally unyielding, breaking down into five distinct classes. At the top were Royalty, Nobility, Knights, Esquires, Gentlemen, and Clergy. Next came the Landholding Commoners (who were not actually landowners), Freeholders (renters of land from which they could never be evicted), Leaseholders, and Copyholders (renters without a lease). Below these came Yeoman (independent renting farmers with about 50 acres of land) and Husbandmen (farmers who often worked as hired laborers). On down the line were Townsfolk, Masters, Journeymen, Apprentices, Laborers, Cottagers, Servants, and lastly the Unemployed Poor. This lowest rung of Elizabethan society consisted of widows, abandoned wives, the non-landowning elderly, and men returning from war. Many such men from Kent eventually found themselves as sailors in ships just like the one Drake later came to captain.

As the son of a non-landowning clergyman, Drake was not of the lowest class, but he certainly held no prospect of ever being considered anyone of rank or name. There is argument that this worked against Drake in later years as he never found himself treated an equal among the gentlemen and naval officers in the Queen's court. There were sneers behind his back even after he became Sir Francis Drake, sneers of which he was surely aware. On the other hand, Drake's lowly birth and rise to the top worked to his advantage in many ways. Most notably, it ensured his connection to the men who served under him.

Drake could be harsh when the situation required it, but his men first and foremost saw him as a man worthy of loyalty. He never led from behind, never avoided hard work, and never kowtowed to the investor gentlemen who often accompanied expeditions. In an age

Francis Drake — Echoes of the Dragon's Drum

when class and title meant everything, Drake found a different way to get everyone's attention: he got results. Even when a mission was an apparent failure, he most often found a way to accomplish more with less than any other captain could imagine. He was brash. He could at times be overconfident. However, he was a self-made man, and those who served under him respected that. On the high seas, respect and loyalty from a crew was essential.

Mre de l'Academie Royale des Sciences
et quelques autres et sur les memoires les plus recens
Par M. de l'Isle

ENTER THE VIRGIN QUEEN – ELIZABETH I (1558-1563)

I know I have the body of a weak and feeble woman, but I have the heart and stomach of a King, and of a King of England too; and think foul scorn that Parma or Spain, or any prince of Europe, should dare to invade the borders of my realm.

—Queen Elizabeth I

It is difficult to overstate the significance that Queen Elizabeth still holds for all English-speaking people. Over four hundred years after her death, the Elizabethan era remains the golden age of England. When she ascended to the throne, hers was the only English-speaking nation in the world. Her island kingdom embraced just over five million people, fewer than either modern-day London or New York. However, a generation later men like Drake, Raleigh, and the colonizers had carried the English language around the world and established their civilization in every quarter of the globe. Within three centuries, English stood as the universal language of commerce, and those living under laws and institutions that found their origins in England had grown a hundredfold.

Nowhere is the lasting nature of Elizabeth's rule more evident than in the single greatest work written in English, the King James Bible (1611). Wood writes: "The goodly heritage that England gave her offspring overseas included Shakespeare and the English Bible. The Authorized Version entered into the very substance of early American life. There was a marked difference between Episcopalian Virginia and Puritan New England. But both took their stand on this version of the English Bible, in which the springs of Holy Writ rejoiced to run through channels of Elizabethan prose. It is true that Elizabeth slept with her fathers before this book of books was printed, and that the first of the Stuarts reigned in her stead. Nevertheless the Authorized Version is pure Elizabethan. All its translators were Elizabethans, as their dedication to King James, still printed with every copy, gratefully acknowledges in its reference to 'the setting of that bright Occidental Star, Queen Elizabeth of most happy memory.'"[16]

More often than not, the Elizabethan era is portrayed as one of discovery, education, wealth, and distinction. No wonder since the likes of Sir Francis Drake, Sir Philip Sidney, Sir Walter Raleigh, Edmund Spenser, Sir John Hawkins, Ben Johnson, Christopher Marlowe, William Shakespeare, Gabriel Harvey, Francis Bacon, and William Camden all flourished during the 44 years of her reign. One need only gaze at the Ditchley portrait of the Queen (1592) that hangs today in the National Portrait Gallery in London to understand the awe she must have inspired in Drake and all others who entered her presence. The portrait gives Elizabeth an almost supernatural aura. Standing against a storm-racked sky giving way to sunshine, she wears a bejeweled white dress; her feet are fixed firmly upon a map of her kingdom; triple the size of England, she towers over Europe; she is stunning, radiant, and tranquilly powerful.

FRANCIS DRAKE ECHOES OF THE DRAGON'S DRUM

But over against that glittering portrait, we should also see England as it really was in Elizabeth's day. For Elizabeth's London still lay closer to the Middle Ages than to the Industrial Revolution, the grimmest reminder of this reality being the prevalence of diseases with no cure. In his excellent work, *Elizabeth's Sea Dogs* (2010), Hugh Bicheno paints a vivid picture of the daily realities of the deadly diseases faced by the people of Francis Drake's time:

> *"Contagious diseases such as smallpox, diphtheria, measles, scarlet fever and chickenpox did dreadful execution among children, and even those with strong immune systems could still be carried off by diseases almost unknown in relatively hygienic modern England. The main scourges were lice-borne typhus; water-borne typhoid, cholera and dysentery (the bloody flux); flea-borne bubonic plague and air-borne pneumonic plague (together, the Black Death); mosquito-borne malaria (the ague); and a 'sweating sickness' (probably influenza) that disappeared after 1578. Tuberculosis was endemic and ergotism, caused by a fungal infection of rye arising from damp storage, added to the misery of scarcity following bad harvests. Open wounds invited deadly septicaemia and tetanus, and virulent syphilis had recently joined long-endemic gonorrhoea among the sexually transmitted diseases."*[17]

In stark contrast to the general uncleanness of the age, there existed a wealthy gentry that gave Elizabethan England the illusion of prosperity unknown to the country as a whole. It is ironic that the Queen said to own a thousand dresses felt constrained to attempt to throttle her subjects' extravagance with her *Statues of Apparel* in 1574. The preamble reads:

FRANCIS DRAKE — ECHOES OF THE DRAGON'S DRUM

"The excess of apparel and the superfluity of unnecessary foreign wares thereto belonging now of late years is grown by sufferance to such an extremity that the manifest decay of the whole realm generally is like to follow by bringing into the realm such superfluities of silks, cloths of gold, silver, and other most vain devices of so great cost for the quantity thereof as of necessity the moneys and treasure of the realm is and must be yearly conveyed out of the same to answer the said excess, but also particularly the wasting and undoing of a great number of young gentlemen, otherwise serviceable, and others seeking by show of apparel to be esteemed as gentlemen, who, allured by the vain show of those things, do not only consume themselves, their goods, and lands which their parents left unto them, but also run into such debts and shifts as they cannot live out of danger of laws without attempting unlawful acts, whereby they are not any ways serviceable to their country as otherwise they might be."[18]

Queen Elizabeth I

Beneath the glittering surface of Elizabeth's England lay a seething cauldron of religious and political intrigue. Steven Alford offers this insight into the precarious nature of Elizabeth's reign:

"Elizabeth's England was in fact anything but stable. There were, after all, few secure foundations for stability. As a family, the Tudors held on to power rather precariously. After the death of Henry VIII in 1547, the English royal succession swerved unexpectedly between all three of Henry's children: a boy too young to rule for himself and two women, one a Catholic, the other a Protestant. Between 1530 and Elizabeth's accession as queen in 1558 Tudor England experienced a political, religious and social revolution. . . These profound changes were punctuated by foreign wars, domestic rebellions, the emergence of corrosive theories of political resistance and for many ordinary men and women, economic misery. In 1558, Queen Elizabeth inherited a shocked and shattered nation.

"It was no wonder that Elizabeth and her government became so adept at masking these harsh realities. Elizabethan propaganda was not a thing of luxury: it was an essential anesthetic. Elizabeth found an empty treasury and a country sick of war. Yet still the revolution continued. Against the conservative inclinations of many of her own people and to the anger of Catholic princes and potentates in Europe, she and her ministers built a Protestant Church modeled upon that of her father and younger brother, in which the queen exercised the authority to govern. Catholics throughout Europe found this proposition both incomprehensible—how could a woman place herself at the head of Christ's Church—and deeply offensive.

FRANCIS DRAKE — ECHOES OF THE DRAGON'S DRUM

"One thing that Elizabeth did not do, famously, was to marry. She resisted practically every effort to find her a husband. Even when a marriage looked possible, the negotiations were scuttled by political and religious reservations. There was no plausible candidate to succeed her. Without either a legitimate heir or a named successor backed by the political elite, England faced ruin. Upon Elizabeth alone rested Protestant England's survival or catastrophe…True, England survived the dynastic ambitions and military might of King Philip of Spain as well as the claim to Elizabeth's throne of a dangerous pretender, Mary, Queen of Scots. One mark of Elizabethan success is that the queen survived to die in her bed in 1603. But it was a near-run thing."[19]

Francis Drake's introduction to the lure of the sea and distaste for all things Roman Catholic coincided with the reign of this Queen.

Henry VIII had been a champion of the navy, but from the time of his death in 1547 to the demise of his daughter Mary in 1558, the total ships in England's navy fell from 80 to 26. Worse yet, during this same time Spain and Portugal expanded their navies exponentially with no plans of slowing down. Not only had old ships not been replaced, but new ships had been sold off at bargain prices for quick cash. As Fowler writes:

"The experiment of a woman ruler had turned out badly. It was hardly to be expected that the sister of the dying Queen would concern herself any more than Mary had done with voyages or navies or other such affairs of the sea. Yet Elizabeth, it was whispered, was her father's daughter. And Henry VIII's unflagging interest and greatest achievement had

FRANCIS DRAKE   ECHOES OF THE DRAGON'S DRUM

been the Navy Royal." Elizabeth came to the throne on November 17, 1558, and from ". . . her political seamanship and undeviating, if zigzag, course would emerge the reality of English seapower."[20]

Elizabeth's ascension to the throne came at an opportune time for England in general and Francis Drake in particular. Here was a queen who understood the value of sea power. Yes, she often allowed King Philip to imagine she would consent to a marriage uniting Spain and England. And she was prone to play the political brinksmanship game in such a way that gave military men heartburn. But first and foremost she loved her country and wanted what was best for her subjects. Francis Drake was just the kind of man she would later need to keep Spain in check. Drake was eighteen when Elizabeth began her forty-four year reign of relative peace. Much of that peace was due to her privately sanctioned, clandestine war waged by her Sea Dogs thousands of miles away.

FRANCIS DRAKE — Echoes of the Dragon's Drum

Drake's Introduction to Exploration with John Hawkins (1564-1569)

O great design!
Ye Sons of Mercy! O complete your work;
Wrench from Oppression's hand the iron rod,
And bid the cruel feel the pains they give.

—Hannah Moore

Modern historians' bias against Francis Drake is nowhere more evident than when it comes to the issue of slavery. It is now in vogue to paint Drake as, first and foremost, a slave trader, and so dismiss the numerous achievements of his life. *Sir Francis Drake: Slave Trader and Pirate* (2009), for example, all but erases Drake's circumnavigation of the earth, his contributions to naval advancement, his relationship to Queen Elizabeth, and his service to England with the broad stroke of implied complicity in the expansion of the slave trade. Worse yet, this is a Scholastic Series book aimed at youth, and so it places Drake alongside the likes of Genghis Kahn, Napoleon, Adolph Hitler, Joseph Stalin, and—what would be to Sir Francis's horror—Mary Queen of Scots.

Most of this association of Drake with slavery is due to his early voyages with his cousin, John Hawkins. Unlike young Drake, the elder Hawkins

FRANCIS DRAKE — ECHOES OF THE DRAGON'S DRUM

deserves the label of slaver. While sailing in the Canaries, Hawkins made plans to enter the slave trade in Guinea. This involved Pedro de Ponte equipping the fleet with supplies, making the needed arrangements with merchants in the Indies, and procuring the skilled pilot necessary to handle navigation. Hawkins in turn would provide the ships and the capital. For Hawkins, his partners, and investors, the goal was entirely profit. To them it was simple economics: prices offered for slaves in the Indies were high and costs for what they saw as chattel were low in Africa. Profits in the slave trade were enormous, and it was not hard to find financial backing.

From his base in London, Hawkins made his preparations for the journey. His father-in-law Benjamin Gonson, treasurer of the navy, took a major role in the syndicate formed to finance the trip. Among the other partners were William Wynter, surveyor of the navy and master of ordnance, and two city magistrates. Led by Hawkins, the fleet of four small ships left Plymouth in October 1562,

Portrait of John Hawkins, National Maritime Museum, London.

FRANCIS DRAKE — ECHOES OF THE DRAGON'S DRUM

manned by a hundred sailors, one of whom was Francis Drake.

Most notable is the fact that this is the first recorded slaving voyage in English history. Between 1562 and 1565, Hawkins commanded two expeditions to Africa, where he acquired a few hundred slaves and sold them to the Spaniards in the West Indies for American produce such as hides and treasure.

No honest appraisal of anyone involved in the slave trade should whitewash what a nasty, though extremely profitable, business it was. From the African warlords who often imprisoned captives for years before selling them, to the Arab middlemen who ruthlessly killed any slave who cost too much to keep alive until buyers came along, to the English investors who were in no way ignorant of where their profits came from, to the ships' captains and crews who transported the hapless souls in their ships' holds, to the Spanish buyers in the New World—all were equally guilty. Slavery was truly an international affair that ensured everyone profited except, of course, the enslaved Africans.

It was an inhuman trade, less offensive to the sometimes duller sensibilities of the 16th century than to us, but nevertheless undeniable in its brutality to all but the most insensitive observer. These objections do not seem to have troubled Hawkins or his backers, who simply asked that the colonial products brought back to Europe reap a sufficient profit. Drake's captain and cousin used two methods to gather his slaves: direct raids upon native villages and the plundering of Portuguese vessels for their Africans. As for the slaving, most Elizabethans regarded the African as less than human and thus exempt from normal consideration. Open

FRANCIS DRAKE   ECHOES OF THE DRAGON'S DRUM

discussion about the morality of the business was rare in England at that time and would be for another 200 years until William Wilberforce finally pricked the national conscience to such an extent that Parliament ended England's participation in the dirty business.

There is hardly a soul alive today who is not horrified and offended by the very idea of human slavery. We seethe with moral indignation at it, and we cannot imagine how anyone or any culture ever approved of it. However, in the world into which Francis Drake was born, the opposite was true. Slavery was as accepted as birth, marriage, and death; it was so woven into the tapestry of human history that it seemed a natural part of it. Everywhere on the globe, for five thousand years, the idea of human civilization without slavery was inconceivable.

Ignorance is no excuse for the inhumanity of slavery, yet one must see Drake and his brief connection with slavery in context. Very few thought to question slavery in those days. While the great Spanish missionary, Las Casas, denounced Spanish atrocities against the Indians, he thought Africans, who could be domesticated, would do as substitutes for Indians, who could not be domesticated. "The Indians," he said, "withered at the white man's touch. The negroes, if properly treated, throve, and were safer than among their enemies at home."[21] Most Europeans did not even consider Africans human and so did not see slavery as inhumane.

Those two centuries following the time of John Hawkins and Francis Drake saw slavery in the West Indies evolve into the cruelest of possible enterprises. The route taken by Hawkins on his slave trading ventures came to be known as the Middle Passage. On the first leg of the slave

FRANCIS DRAKE — ECHOES OF THE DRAGON'S DRUM

trade, European goods were transported to Africa and there unloaded; on the second, the ship was filled with its human cargo, who during this "middle passage" were transported to the West Indies, to be sold there; and on its final leg the ship carried West Indian goods back to Europe. One famous account of the Middle Passage comes via a ship's surgeon, Alexander Falconbridge, who described in vivid detail the dreadful picture of the slave trade:

> "The hardships and inconveniences suffered by the Negroes during the passage are scarcely to be enumerated or conceived. They are far more violently affected by seasickness than Europeans. It frequently terminates in death, especially among the women. But the exclusion of fresh air is among the most intolerable. For the purpose of admitting this needful refreshment, most of the ships in the slave trade are provided, between the decks, with five or six air-ports on each side of the ship, of about five inches in length and four in breadth. But whenever the sea is rough and the rain heavy it becomes necessary to shut these and every other conveyance by which the air is admitted. The fresh air being thus excluded, the Negroes' rooms soon grow intolerable hot. The confined air, rendered noxious by the effluvia exhaled from their bodies and being repeatedly breathed, soon produces fevers and [diarrhea] which generally carries off great numbers of them…But the excessive heat was not the only thing that rendered their situation intolerable. The deck, that is the floor of their rooms, was so covered with the blood and mucus which had proceeded from them in consequence of the [diarrhea], that it resembled a slaughter-house. It is not in the power of the human imagination to picture a situation more dreadful or disgusting… The place allotted for the sick Negroes is under the half deck, where they lie

on the bare planks. By this means those who are emaciated frequently have their skin and even their flesh entirely rubbed off, by the motion of the ship, from the prominent parts of the shoulders, elbows and hips so as to render the bones quite bare. And some of them, by constantly lying in the blood and mucus that had flowed from those afflicted with the flux and which is generally so violent as to prevent their being kept clean, having their flesh much sooner rubbed off than those who have only to contend with the mere friction of the ship. The excruciating pain which the poor sufferers feel from being obliged to continue in such a dreadful situation, frequently for several weeks, in case they happen to live so long, is not to be conceived or described."[22]

This is not to say that that Europeans had not begun to be troubled by the manner in which both slaves and Native Americans were being treated in the New World. The Spanish Conquistadors proved exceptionally treacherous in their treatment of the native population in both Central and South America to the point that even some priests and other Spaniards began to raise questions. As Sugden writes: "There is no reason to suppose that sensitive men can have been blind to the sufferings of the African natives they kidnapped and herded on to foul hulks for personal profit. Drake was in his twenties and did not question what his elders accepted, but he must share the blame, although in him, at least, there dwelt a capacity to sympathize with the blacks which time would one day draw out."[23]

Present day biographers miss one of the great hallmarks of Drake's character because they insist on focusing on his early slave trading days while under the tutelage of his cousin, John Hawkins. That trait so often

FRANCIS DRAKE   ECHOES OF THE DRAGON'S DRUM

overlooked today is the compassion he displayed toward both slave and enemy. Hawkins continued in the slave trade for years, but Drake turned his attention to exploration and, of course, making himself a thorn in the side of Spain anywhere he could. Through all of those exploits, Francis Drake displayed an understanding of the equality of men that mystified other leaders, garnered intense loyalty from his crew, and earned him the grudging admiration of even his worst enemy.

Ernle Bradford describes this quality of Drake in his fine little biography, *The Wind Commands Me* (1965): "He was far in advance of his age in his humanity and compassion. His treatment of Spanish prisoners, his conduct towards Negroes and American Indians and his consideration towards his sailors mark him as exceptional in his own age, and still worthy of emulation in ours. As a seaman he was the first to realize that there could be no distinction of caste or class aboard ship, but that 'the gentleman must haul and draw with the mariner, and the mariner with the gentleman.' He thus anticipated by some 400 years the democratic navies of today. If England had taken his lesson properly to hand, she would've had a far more efficient fleet in the first half of the 20th century."[24]

The first trip that Drake made with Hawkins involved trading African slaves to work on Spanish plantations in South America in exchange for goods to take back to England. Their first trading expedition was a great success, so Hawkins and Drake returned the following year in 1568. But this second trip was not destined to go quite so well. While resupplying at the port of San Juan de Ulúa, Drake and Hawkins were attacked by a fleet of Spanish warships and lost all but two of their ships and most

FRANCIS DRAKE   ECHOES OF THE DRAGON'S DRUM

their crew. Drake and Hawkins escaped by swimming away during the chaos and made their way back separately to England.

On their return, Hawkins and Drake found England, France, and Spain on the verge of all-out war. Just when Queen Elizabeth thought she had managed to avoid confrontation with the much stronger Spain, the news of the happenings at Ulúa brought by the two upset the delicate balance of peace. William Wood explains:

> "William Hawkins, John's brother, wrote a petition to the Queen-in-Council for letters-of-marque in reprisal for Ulua, and Drake dashed off for London with the missive almost before the ink was dry. Now it happened that a Spanish treasure fleet, carrying money from Italy and bound for Antwerp, had been driven into Plymouth and neighboring ports by Huguenot privateers. This money was urgently needed by Alva, the very capable but ruthless governor of the Spanish Netherlands. . . . The Spanish ambassador therefore obtained leave to bring it overland to Dover. But no sooner had Elizabeth signed the order of safe conduct than in came Drake with the news of San Juan de Ulua."[25]

The die was cast. Elizabeth, always wavering between war and peace, knew she would not be able to keep her Sea Dogs in check without allowing reprisal for the unwarranted attack on Hawkins expedition. Wood continues, "Elizabeth at once saw that all the English sea-dogs would be flaming for revenge. Everyone saw that the treasure would be safer now in England than aboard any Spanish vessel in the Channel. So, on the ground that the gold, though payable to Philip's representative in Antwerp, was still the property of the Italian bankers who advanced it, Elizabeth sent orders down post-haste to commandeer it. The enraged ambassador advised Alva to seize everything English in the Netherlands. Elizabeth in turn seized everything Spanish in England. Elizabeth now held the diplomatic trumps; for existing treaties provided that there should be no reprisals without a reasonable delay; and Alva had seized English property before giving Elizabeth the customary time to explain."[26]

For John Hawkins, reprisal was simply a business proposition, but for Drake, it was personal. There would be a brief pause in his life for his marriage to Mary Newman in 1569, but while Hawkins was content to become admiral of the royal naval yard, Drake would soon be heading back to the West Indies. Slave trading was a momentary blip in his life, but reprisal on the Spanish became life-long obsession.

M. DE L'ACADEMIE ROYALE des SCIENCES
et quelques autres et sur les memoires les plus recens
PAR M. DE L'ISLE

FRANCIS DRAKE — ECHOES OF THE DRAGON'S DRUM

PRIVATEER OR PIRATE

Oh, the privateer
The sea-dog's reamed in legends, it said he had the second sight
His assignment must be holy, he fought the fight with power and pride
The key to ancient wisdom, the power to have seen the truth
He'll return to holy ground, where his tortured soul had died in youth
His all-seeing spy-glass is aiming at the sea
No mariner has the slightest chance to flee
His Crystal-ball's revealing where he has to steer
He fights the covered evil without fear
Oh, the privateer

—Rolf Kasparek

Ironically, when John Hawkins made his initial expeditions he had no intention of plundering Spanish treasures or interloping on their territory. He came as a businessman intending to trade with the fledgling Spanish colonies in the New World. Their mother country saw the matter differently. Throughout this period, Spain considered those who profited on its New World possessions to be interlopers. Once the *Treaty of Tordesillas* was signed in 1484, "no peace beyond this line" became Spain's guiding principle for dealing with all non-Spanish ships sighted in what they considered their possession. As far as King Philip was concerned, John Hawkins and anyone else he did

FRANCIS DRAKE   ECHOES OF THE DRAGON'S DRUM

not sanction trading beyond the line was a pirate and should be dealt with accordingly.

This is one of the reasons that constructing an accurate telling of Francis Drake's story is so difficult. Angus Konstam in his excellent work, *Pirates* (2008), explains how murky the waters of international exploration and trade in that era could be:

> "There really is some truth in the idea that one country's privateer is another country's pirate. This famously swashbuckling age of the Elizabethan sea dogs, Spanish treasure galleons and daredevil raids on the Spanish Main was a time when national and individual interests could be pursued in tandem, and a fortune could be won while ostensibly serving the state. For much of this period Catholic Spain and Protestant England, while not exactly at war with each other, were rivals. While this undeclared war continued, rulers, diplomats, and sea captains had to tread a fine line between taking advantage of the hostility and overstepping political and diplomatic boundaries."[27]

The Elizabethan Sea Dogs never considered themselves to be pirates and by all existing standards of their day, their belief was well founded. Pirates knew no rules, plundered wherever and whomever they pleased, and answered to no one but themselves. Privateers were part of a well-established, though somewhat clandestine, enterprise covered by generally agreed upon rules. John Hawkins, Francis Drake, and those in their fraternity were considered independent contractors in the service of their country, and they were allowed to take a healthy profit for their troubles. Later Drake always carried with him a legal document known

FRANCIS DRAKE — ECHOES OF THE DRAGON'S DRUM

as a letter of marque that in effect made him a licensed pirate. That document meant that Drake was under the qualified protection of the country he sailed for with contractual obligation to share a healthy percentage of profits from his raids in the Spanish Main and beyond. Without these letters of marque and the Sea Dogs that operated under them, England had no hope of exploration, colonization, or trade.

As long as the privateers abided by the rules and attacked only the enemies of the state listed on their letter of marque, privateers could not be hanged as pirates, condemned to a lifetime of servitude in the galleys, or simply killed outright. Other nations recognized this operating principle, but not the Spanish. For most of his adult life Francis Drake was a privateer operating for profit "beyond the line" in the service of his Queen. In our day he would be considered the equivalent of some clandestine government operative, gathering vital intelligence, crippling the enemy when he could, and providing those who approved his mission with plausible deniability.

When an English ship operating with a letter of marque was attacked, that ship's captain often requested a letter of reprisal giving him official sanction to recover what was stolen from him and gain recompense for lost ships and men. After Hawkins's problems with the Spanish, Queen Elizabeth issued him a letter of reprisal that allowed him to attack Spanish shipping and property as a means of redress for the losses he suffered at the hands of the Spanish. The English (as well as the French and Dutch) considered reprisal a perfectly legal act, which effectively bestowed privateering status upon these raiders. Francis Drake saw the rest of his life as a continuous reprisal against Spain.

FRANCIS DRAKE — ECHOES OF THE DRAGON'S DRUM

In truth, most of the navies of the world were a mixture of civilian and government enterprise in the 16th century. Our modern concept of military sea power does not fit the reality of Francis Drake's world. European nations had been depending on mercenary navies as well as armies for centuries before Drake followed his cousin to the Spanish Main, and this would continue to be the norm for three hundred years after. England, in particular, elevated the private navy and privateers to a level unseen in the rest of Europe. "Whereas . . . foreign hirelings rarely received compensation for loss or damage in the state's service, with the result that they were highly reluctant and undependable combatants, there developed in England a tradition of recompense for repair the ship owners had not willingly let die."[28]

When most people today hear the term "pirate," they immediately imagine peg-legged, parrot-toting characters with exotic names such as Blackbeard, "Calico Jack" Rackman, and "Gentleman" Steed Bonnet. In truth, almost everything we moderns know of pirates is from a period (1690–1730) sometimes called the Golden Age of Piracy. Hollywood and literature have focused almost exclusively on the image invoked by this handful of pirates making them either romantic saviors or grotesque villains. Much of this image is the work of pure pirate fiction rather than fact. The vast majority of pirates were merely sailors who rebelled against a vicious and oppressive system of labor. A great number of such men began their life on the sea as legitimate sailors, pressed into service and treated with less respect than the cargo they carried. The romantic view of piracy disregards the fact that conditions were still harsh, that fever and disease were commonplace, and that life expectancy was measured more in months than years.

FRANCIS DRAKE   ECHOES OF THE DRAGON'S DRUM

Putting aside all such misconceptions, it is settled fact that while England came to consider Drake a national hero, Spain considered him the 16th century's most notorious pirate. Referred to as "the main cause of wars" in one 1592 letter to King Philip II, Drake so harassed Spanish ships in two oceans and was so despised by the Spanish that Philip II placed what amounted to a 7 million dollar bounty on his head. Given that Spanish accounts told of a captain who attacked and boarded Spanish merchant ships to steal their treasure and make off with it in the kind of arrogant and dramatic way that have become standard fare in pirate lore, this comes as no surprise.

History is often a matter of comparisons. Francis Drake captured individual ships, took what he believed was owed him in recompense, and more often than not set his captives free (unless, of course, they crossed him too severely). By modern standards, some of his actions appear barbarous, but not to 16th century observers. The Spanish was hardly above using privateers and piracy themselves. As one English writer would later put it, "The Spaniards had carried barbarism to such a pitch in seizing our ships and condemning their crews to the galleys, that Queen Elizabeth was never averse to meeting murder and plunder by more than the equivalent in retaliation." [29]

Ten years before Francis Drake was born, the conquistador Francisco Pizarro set the bar for comparison of what was ethical and what was not. From 1530 to 1532, Pizarro probed the outskirts of the Inca Empire, conquering and recruiting allies along the way. The defining moment in Pizarro's conquest of the Incas came with the capture of Emperor Atahualpa in 1532. Compared to Atahualpa's thousands of Incan

FRANCIS DRAKE   ECHOES OF THE DRAGON'S DRUM

warriors, Pizarro had less than 200 men. However, the Conquistador's advantage of firearms, cannon, and horses made him an unstoppable force. By best accounts, Pizarro sent a priest to speak first to the Incan emperor. A priest, Vicente, approached Atahualpa with a Bible and said: "I am a priest of God, and I teach Christians the things of God, and in like manner I come to teach you. What I teach is that which God says to us in this Book. Therefore, on the part of God and of the Christians, I beseech you to be their friend, for such is God's will, and it will be for your good. Go and speak to the Governor, who waits for you." In essence, Vicente was telling Atahualpa that resistance was useless. Atahualpa asked to see the Bible, opened it, and then tossed it aside saying, "I know well how you have behaved on the road, how you have treated my chiefs, and taken the cloth from my storehouses . . . I will not leave this place until they bring it all to me."[30]

Francisco Pizarro.

Upon his refusal, the great Atahualpa was taken captive. The Incan emperor assumed that he would be killed if the invaders did not get what they wanted, namely gold. He was partly right. Gold was a primary motivation for the Spaniards in the New World, but they also wanted their land. Reliable reports from the incident showed that Atahualpa converted to Catholicism that day, but was still put to death. Read anything about the inquisitions of the Church in Europe, and you will find very similar accounts. Non-Christians or Christians believed to be heretics were rounded up and commanded to repent. Depending on the crime, the accused could be executed even if he did repent. The penalty for those that did not repent was execution by burning. In 1533, the Incan capital of Cuzco fell to the Spaniards. The conquest then continued until Spain controlled all of Mexico, Central America, and South America (except Brazil).

One of the books that Francis Drake carried with him on his later voyages was his prized Foxe's *Book of Martyrs*. His childhood was filled with stories of religious persecution and papal atrocities. He and his fellow Sea Dogs had no great love for the Spanish and their ways, but his was a special distrust. Had anyone called him a pirate in comparison with the Spanish Conquistadors, he would have surely responded with genuine shock and disdain.

Even if one considers Francis Drake a pirate, as every loyal Spaniard did, his life and character left no doubt that his figure was cut from a different cloth. As one biographer put it, Drake was a strict disciplinarian who "would have no gambling with cards or dice aboard his ship, did not tolerate foul talk, would not have his crew hanging about bars and brothels when ashore. Such a man might well have been unpopular, but we have it on record (from Spanish prisoners among others) that he was loved by his men. He had an infectious vitality, humor, and resilient character."[31] There is no doubt he had his faults, as we will see later in his

FRANCIS DRAKE   ECHOES OF THE DRAGON'S DRUM

story, but whatever they were, his strength of character and connection to those who sailed under him always won the day.

As Drake sailed home from his first adventures in the New World, he hardly returned as a notable success. He had seen hopes of profit and national pride wither before superior Spanish gunfire; he had seen English ships sunk, with little but his life to show for the effort. He had seen good friends die—as far as he knew, his mentor and cousin John Hawkins, among them. Francis Drake sailed home as a minor figure whose name was forgotten even by those he fought against. When captured by the Spanish, an English seaman named Noah Sargeant was asked to name the captains in Hawkins's expedition. Drake was not mentioned.

The voyage was an unmitigated disaster. What few assets Drake possessed were invested in a venture that was both a commercial and naval failure. Prospects of other patronage were now doubtful. To most eyes, it appeared Drake might well suffer the same fate as the rotting ship he was raised in. But for Francis, his sorry trip across the Atlantic became a crossroads in his life. During the return voyage, the narrative of Drake's life became the focused story by which we now know him. Before his first journey to the Spanish Main, Drake's life had been forged by his father's stories of flight from Roman Catholic insurgents in Devon and memories of the reign of King Philip in Spain and Queen Mary's bloody reign in England. His family and Protestant background left him with no liking for the enemies of his country and faith. Along with his shipmates aboard the *Jesus*, he denounced the pope, and now

FRANCIS DRAKE   ECHOES OF THE DRAGON'S DRUM

bitter loss and disappointment sharpened his resolve to confront his enemy wherever it might be.

Francis Drake the fledgling trader and potential slaver would be no more. Others might aspire to such lesser goals, but not he. As Sugden puts it: "For the rest of his life Francis Drake pictured himself an avenger, bent upon rewarding the treachery of Don Martin Enriquez. It must have seemed a futile, an almost presumptuous decision at the time, but it put a fire into the obscure little sea captain, defeated and dishonoured. On the pitching *Judith*, brooding upon his misfortunes, Francis Drake declared war upon the King of Spain."[32]

Before his failed expedition with Hawkins, Drake was one among many, a seeker of fame and fortune, one of the Plymouth men doing what all Plymouth men did: live by the lure and rule of the sea. But very soon every Spanish colonial magistrate and sea captain would need ask no one whom they should fear. Francis Drake of Devon was about to spread his wings and be known by another name. He was no longer just the son of an itinerate preacher or cousin of a successful slaver. Nor was he destined to be forgotten in a system where name and lineage was all that seemed to matter. Soon English nobleman would grumble about a commoner who had the ear of the Queen and Spanish mothers would warn their children to be good or suffer the terror of El Draque, Francis Drake the Dragon.

PART III

THE DRAGON SPREADS HIS WINGS

M.rs de l'Academie Royale des Sciences
et quelques autres et sur les memoires les plus recens
Par M. de L'Isle

FRANCIS DRAKE   ECHOES OF THE DRAGON'S DRUM

Great golden galleons plied the Main;
He hit them hard, again, again;
And with his fleet of British ship
Forever broke Spain's tyrant grip.

—Fiske

The Dragon that over seas did raise his crest
And brought back heaps of gold into his nest;
Unto his foes more terrible than thunder,
Glory of his age, after-ages' wonder.

—Robert Hayman

During Mary's reign, the Royal Navy had been neglected to the point that it seemed Elizabeth had little hope of protecting her land and interests. Yet others not so illustrious rose to fill the gap. Fighting traders, privateers, and pirates multiplied in seaports where hatred for Mary, Philip, papal Rome, and the Spanish Inquisition waxed hot. Many of the men who rose to prominence as mercenaries for the Queen came from these seaports.

Queen Elizabeth's Sea Dogs were an unlikely band of full-time opportunists and part-time warriors. Some of their names are familiar; others are veiled in the mists of time. Among them was Sir Walter Raleigh, the dashing aristocrat who searched in futility for the mythical El Dorado, rose to the heights of favor with Elizabeth, fell from it under King James I, and lost his head to the executioner in

FRANCIS DRAKE ECHOES OF THE DRAGON'S DRUM

1618. Others included Thomas Cavendish, who attempted, but failed to circumnavigate the world and died at sea at the age of thirty-two; Humphrey Gilbert, who went down with his ship within sight of the famous *Golden Hind*; Martin Frobisher, who brought back thousands of pounds of ore from Newfoundland only to later discover that what had been sacrificed in term of lives and investment of sponsors was all for two ship loads of iron pyrite; John Hawkins, remembered most for making slaves a chief source of income; and of course, his second cousin and protégée, Francis Drake. In the thirteen years following 1567—when he and Hawkins lost their ships and barely escaped with their lives in the Spanish Main—Drake rose to become the greatest of Elizabeth's Sea Dogs. In 1580 she knighted him Sir Francis.

It is always hard to know if we should believe all the press about our public heroes. Do they really live up to their public persona? The answer is, hardly ever. But the overall picture of a man tells us much we can rely on. Did Ronald Reagan or Winston Churchill ever lie? Yes. But can we know much about their character from the total course of their lives? Absolutely. The same is true for Francis Drake. By the beginning of this period of his life, his reputation grew larger than life. Drake had fast become a symbol of an island nation that had something of an inferiority complex thanks to Portugal and Spain. While the English still puttered around in their channel, Magellan had sailed around the world and Spain's Armada waxed invincible. In short, England needed a hero and Drake was ready for the role.

Here was a commoner, born far removed from the aristocracy and wealth of a Raleigh or a Cavendish, who had become what in another century

Francis Drake — Echoes of the Dragon's Drum

would have been the perfect model for a Horatio Alger novel. He was the poor boy, raised in the rotting hulk of a derelict ship, who became hero to his people and El Draco to his enemies. Early biographers like William Wood describe the Francis Drake of this era as heroic, almost iconic. Wood describes Elizabeth's favored Sea Dog: "Drake was only of medium stature. But he had the strength of a giant, the pluck of a bulldog, the spring of a tiger, and the cut of a man that is born to command. Broad-browed, with steel-blue eyes and close-cropped auburn hair and beard, he was all kindliness of countenance to friends, but a very 'Dragon' to his Spanish foes."[33]

The next two years of Francis Drake's life set the stage for everything that came after. Though his first voyages as captain of his own expeditions proved only moderately successful, they nevertheless promised greater things to come. John Hawkins remained content to reside in Plymouth and assume the role of businessman and admiral of the royal naval yard, but Drake could not wait to head back to the Spanish Main.

et quelques autres et sur les mémoires les plus récens
PAR M. DE L'ISLE

Francis Drake — Echoes of the Dragon's Drum

Drake in the Spanish Main (1572-1573)

And in your fighting evermore, think you are Englishmen,
Then every one of you I hope will slay of Spaniards ten,
Or any else whatever they be, that shall disturb your peace
And seek by any kind of mean your quiet to decease.

—Henry Roberts

John Hawkins brought slaves to trade with the Spanish, who needed them to work their sugar cane plantations. That was a profitable business indeed. But when his cousin, Francis Drake, began to plan his return to the Spanish Main, his eyes rested on a bigger prize. Between Cortes with the Aztecs and Pizarro with the Incas, Spain now held access to the gold that Drake's Queen desperately needed. By the mid-1500s Spain controlled most of Central and South America, the single major source of wealth in the world. Drake understood that his voyages to the New World were no longer simply about adventure or establishing new colonies to establish trade. King Philip had his eyes on total domination of Europe, including the British Isles, and this kind of wealth all but ensured he would soon be able to accomplish that goal. Queen Elizabeth needed that capital, and Drake longed for both his share of plunder and something more. He was determined to get retribution.

One need only look at the target of Drake's first solo voyage to see that he

FRANCIS DRAKE   ECHOES OF THE DRAGON'S DRUM

wanted to deliver a damaging blow to Spain's pipeline of gold, diamonds, and silver. Just over 30 years before this, the Spanish government settled on a method of transport for their wealth that continued well into the eighteenth century. Every year, when the Atlantic hurricane season (July through November) ended, two treasure fleets left the port of Seville in Spain for the New World. One fleet, the Flota, sailed for Vera Cruz by way of the Antilles and Santo Domingo. The other, the Galeones, sailed from Seville to the South American coast where it made its way northward, loading treasure from colonial ports along the way. Perhaps the most important stop in that route was at Nombre de Dios, the narrowest portion of the Isthmus of Panama.

While Spanish gold ships could have sailed southward and rounded South America at Cape Horn, no sea captain wanted to risk the treacherous Strait of Magellan twice a year and no Spanish overlord dared the chance of seeing the King's gold sunk by the dangerous currents. Bullion refined from the mines of the Andes was sent northward by sea to the west coast of Panama and then transported overland by mule to Nombre de Dios. The two treasure fleets then rejoined at Vera Cruz, made their way through the Florida Straits and hastened to beat the worst of the hurricane season before returning to Seville.

As long as storms or accidents did not scatter the fleet, it remained unassailable. The massive galleons of Spain dwarfed the English ships of Drake and the Sea Dogs. They ranged up to 1,000 tons, were floating castles bristling with cannon, and carried a crew of some 200 soldiers and sailors. One ship alone was more than a match for any vessel that might challenge it. Together, the treasure fleet faced no real threat save

FRANCIS DRAKE   ECHOES OF THE DRAGON'S DRUM

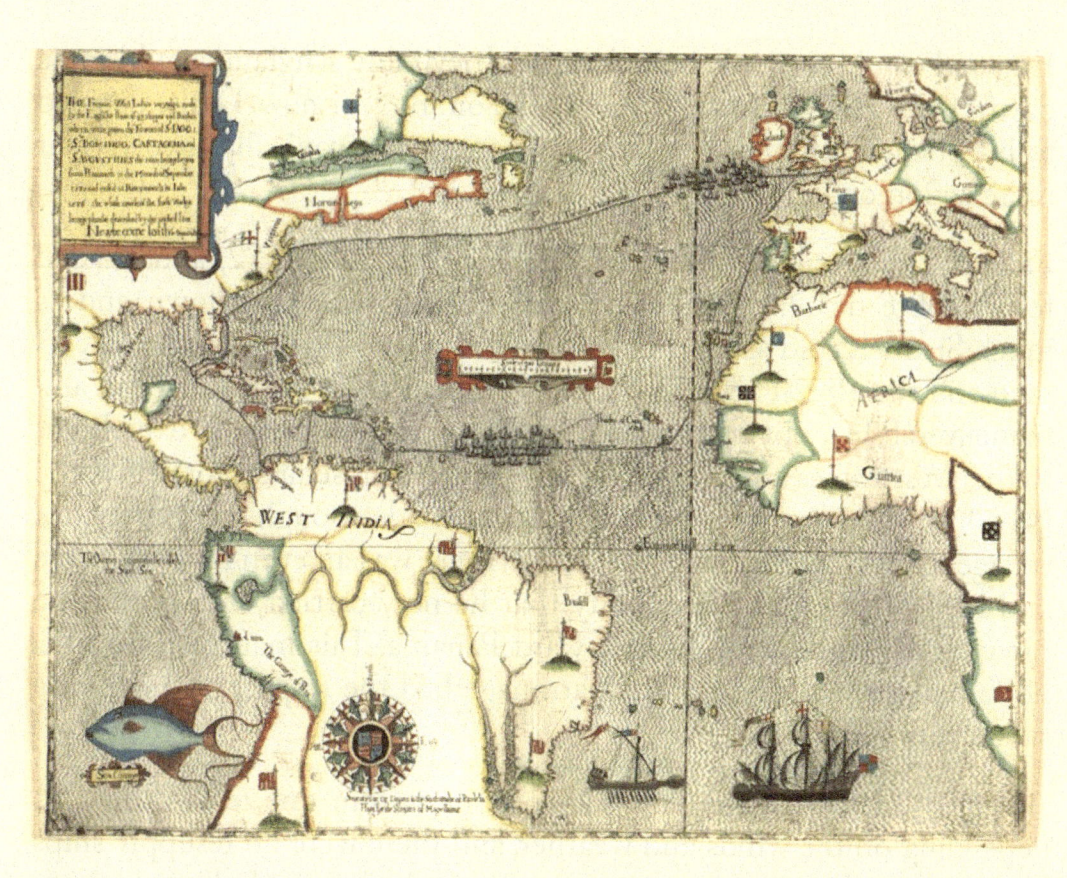

Sir Francis Drake's West Indian Voyage.

from a national navy of comparable size, and their captains knew no such adversary existed.

Storm clouds loomed across the Atlantic, and Elizabeth wisely held out for peace all the while authorizing letters of marque and writs of retribution. Drake's expedition was in essence a surveillance mission, but striking a crippling blow to Spain and bringing some of its gold back to

FRANCIS DRAKE   ECHOES OF THE DRAGON'S DRUM

England would certainly be welcomed. Inevitably, England would some day face the mighty Spanish Navy head on. But for now, Drake decided to hit Spain a different way. This new approach, ironically, involved far more action on land than by sea.

Francis Drake sailed from Plymouth on May 24, 1572, and headed for Nombre de Dios, where he planned to capture the town and as much Spanish gold as he could get his hands on. With him, he took 73 men and the *Pascha* and the *Swan*, two small ships built for speed and maneuverability, not fighting. Drake had returned from an expedition to the West Indies a year earlier with what any subsequent foray into the New World required—capital. Drake also made enough on his previous voyage to own his first ship, the *Swan*. There was an even more valuable and hard to come by commodity that he now carried with him as he directed the *Swan* and *Pascha* toward Panama. This man with no title, no family fortune, and limited patronage had the respect of those who sailed with him.

A sea-voyage across the Atlantic could last from one to two months depending on the winds and weather, and there were no resupply ships like those modern navies enjoy. Provisions had to include everything required for both the trip and the assault on Nombre de Dios. That meant ensuring there was enough water, food, spare sails, spare spars, spare ropes, nails, pitch, tar, gunpowder, shot, cargo, medical supplies, clothing, candles, coal, timber, and oil.

Sailors cannot sail and soldiers cannot fight without nourishment, and proper food supplies often proved a problem. With no modern

FRANCIS DRAKE — ECHOES OF THE DRAGON'S DRUM

refrigeration, preventing food-spoilage was a major issue onboard ships. The *Pascha* and the *Swan* left loaded down with salted pork, dried and salted fish, cornmeal and oats, and drinks that included barrels of water, wine, rum, and grog. The universally despised yet necessary hard-tack was always present on ships of the day. Hard-tack was a special kind of biscuit baked so that when it came out of the oven, it was rock hard. It was notoriously challenging to eat but if sealed properly and kept dry, this life sustaining provision could be kept fresh for months and even years at sea. Since the stuff could well break off teeth, sailors often dunked their hard-tack in coffee or tea to soften it.

One nutritional challenge that caused constant problems was the lack of greenery. Vegetables and fruit could not be salted and only lasted a few days aboard ship before going bad. Islands of any kind were sparse on the trans-Atlantic voyage, so sailors often went weeks with none of the essential nutrients found in greens. However, variety in diet was not the chief concern when it came to this missing ingredient. Too long without it and the dreaded disease scurvy was bound to follow. Symptoms of the disease were unmistakable. It caused joints to ache, gums to bleed, and teeth to rot and fall out. Sailors with scurvy also were not of much use in fighting since it left them dizzy, weak, and faint. To prevent this, sailors drank inordinate quantities of fruit-juice. As a result British sailors came to be called "Limeys" for the gallons of lime juice they drank.

These were small ships with very limited space. Drake and perhaps a first mate had a small cabin, but everyone else from officer to Gentleman to deck hand slept in hammocks on and below deck. Hammocks were

FRANCIS DRAKE — ECHOES OF THE DRAGON'S DRUM

used because they required little space, and one was less likely to be pitched out of the cocoon-like hammock than a bed. Naval tradition dictated that when a sailor died, he was sewn up in his hammock (with the last stitch through his nose, to ensure he wasn't simply sound asleep). Sailors tied the dead crewman's ankles with a pair of holystones (a type of scouring-rock used to clean the deck) and tipped his body into the sea.

Open flames were forbidden on sailing-ships. The only source of light was fire, and its use was strictly regulated. All candles had to be housed in lanterns for extra safety, and the only fire permitted onboard was in the galley stove. Most ships had a stern lantern (a big lantern hammered onto the back of the ship) to act a bit like the taillight of a car. When escaping an enemy ship, captains usually doused their stern lantern to remain hidden in the dark.

In spite of all the hardships of the voyage, however, the *Pascha* and the *Swan* arrived safely at Nombre de Dios in July, ready to begin a new phase in England's unofficial challenge to Spain's domination of the New World. Drake's target was the most significant port for shipping in all of the Americas. Located on the Atlantic coast of Panama, Nombre de Dios made a logical place for Drake to begin his campaign in the Spanish Main since it was a major port of call for the Spanish treasure fleet. Twice a year, Peruvian silver shipped to Panama was transported by mule rain across the isthmus to Nombre de Dios for shipment to Cuba and Spain. Drake wanted retribution for the losses caused to him by the Spanish a few years earlier, and there was no better place to start.

William Wood describes the ensuing battle vividly:

FRANCIS DRAKE — ECHOES OF THE DRAGON'S DRUM

"Springing eagerly ashore the Englishmen tumbled the Spanish guns off their platforms while the astonished sentry ran for dear life. In five minutes the church bells were pealing out their wild alarms, trumpet calls were sounding, drums were beating round the general parade, and the civilians of the place, expecting massacre at the hands of the Maroons, were rushing about in agonized confusion. Drake's men fell in—they were all well-drilled—and were quickly told off into three detachments. The largest under Drake, the next under Oxenham—the hero of Kingsley's Westward Ho!—and the third, of twelve men only, to guard the pinnaces. Having found that the new fort on the hill commanding the town was not yet occupied, Drake and Oxenham marched against the town at the head of their sixty men, Oxenham by a flank, Drake straight up the main street, each with a trumpet sounding, a drum rolling, fire-pikes blazing, swords flashing, and all ranks yelling like fiends. . . .

"As Drake's men reached the Plaza, his trumpeter blew one blast of defiance and then fell dead. Drake returned the Spanish volley and charged immediately, the drummer beating furiously, pikes leveled, and swords brandished. The Spaniards did not wait for him to close; for Oxenham's party, fire-pikes blazing, were taking them in flank. Out went the Spaniards through the Panama gate, with screaming townsfolk scurrying before them. Bang went the gate, now under English guard, as Drake made for the Governor's house. There lay a pile of silver bars such as his men had never dreamt of: in all, about four hundred tons of silver ready for the homeward fleet— enough not only to fill but sink the Pascha, Swan, and pinnaces. But silver was then no more to Drake than it was once to Solomon. What he wanted were the

FRANCIS DRAKE — ECHOES OF THE DRAGON'S DRUM

diamonds and pearls and gold, which were stored, he learned, in the King's Treasure House beside the bay.

"A terrific storm now burst. The fire-pikes and arquebuses had to be taken under cover. The wall of the King's Treasure House defied all efforts to breach it. And the Spaniards who had been shut into the town, discovering how few the English were, reformed for attack. Some of Drake's men began to lose heart. But in a moment he stepped to the front and ordered Oxenham to go round and smash in the Treasure House gate while he held the Plaza himself. Just as the men stepped off, however, he reeled aside and fell. He had fainted from loss of blood caused by a wound he had managed to conceal. There was no holding the men now. They gave him a cordial, after which he bound up his leg, for he was a first-rate surgeon, and repeated his orders as before. But there were a good many wounded; and, with Drake no longer able to lead, the rest all begged to go back. So back to their boats they went, and over to the Bastimentos or Victualling Islands, which contained the gardens and poultry runs of the Nombre de Dios citizens."[34]

Drake's assault on Nombre de Dios proved nothing short of disastrous. All began well as the raiders destroyed the harbor's guns without incident and proceeded to capture the royal storehouse. But from there things went downhill quickly. They had missed the treasure fleet by a few weeks; the gold was gone. His men, untrained in land warfare, panicked in the darkness as they discovered their leader had suffered from a musket ball shot to the leg. When he collapsed from loss of blood, everyone evacuated to Port Pheasant with nothing to show for

FRANCIS DRAKE   ECHOES OF THE DRAGON'S DRUM

their effort save a small merchantman loaded with Spanish wine, a dead compatriot, and a severely wounded commander.

To make matters worse yet, all hope for surprise evaporated with the failed raid. As word spread, local authorities rushed to protect their property from the English marauders. A few days later, when the now recovering Drake raided Cartagena, he found a single coasting vessel in the harbor which Spanish horsemen were more than ready to protect from English looting. The following day two small Spanish boats were

Sir Francis Drake in Cartagena 1585.

FRANCIS DRAKE — ECHOES OF THE DRAGON'S DRUM

captured, but contained no silver or gold. And then Drake lost his prized *Swan*. Though he sought to point blame elsewhere, most chroniclers see solid evidence that Drake did not want to tarnish the family name by naming the captain of the *Swan* responsible for the loss since that meant bringing charges against his younger brother, John.

There was additional raiding along the mainland, but it produced little in the way of wealth. With Spanish pressure increasing, Drake abandoned Port Pheasant and built a new camp, Fort Diego, on an island in late September or early October. Drake split his raiding forces then between himself and his brother John. Again, he met disaster. Francis returned to the fort a few weeks later, still without plunder, to find a Spanish arrow had mortally wounded his brother. It was a dark time, but in it another character trait of Drake's became apparent: persistence. Though despondent, Drake resolved to wait on the island until the Spanish treasure fleet returned the following spring.

For a time, Drake's men rested, played, and recuperated. But then a more formidable enemy than the Spanish appeared. As in most wars, this enemy claimed more lives than any sword, arrow, cannon shot, bullet, or bomb ever would. While the men waited for the treasure ships to return the dreaded vómito negro slipped into camp and struck with a vengeance. The yellow fever that plagued Europeans in the Americas for the next three hundred years introduced itself and quickly decimated Drake's men. In a matter of days, most of the men grew sick and many died, including Drake's brother, Joseph. The ones who survived remained weakened for weeks, and many in all likelihood never fully recovered. 72 men sailed from Plymouth in May of 1572; only half now survived.

FRANCIS DRAKE — ECHOES OF THE DRAGON'S DRUM

Francis Drake knew only one direction in life: forward. All he needed was some fresh manpower to press his campaign forward. Ironically, though he had been on the crew of slave ship for a short time under his cousin, escaped slaves came to his rescue. Through a slave freed in the raid on Nombre de Dios, Drake managed to befriend a local band of Cimarrons—black Africans who had escaped their Spanish masters. Drake and these Cimarrons had one thing in common—their hatred of the Spanish. In fact, though such seemed impossible, these Africans who had escaped from Spanish plantations and mines held more grievances against the Spaniards than even Francis Drake. The Cimarrons—called "feral cattle" by the Spanish—had intermarried with the Amerindians and established free communities in the jungle. From these they waged merciless guerrilla warfare against their former masters. Drake and the Cimarrons made a perfect match.

Some biographers label Drake lucky and others an opportunist. Whatever the label, Drake knew how to seize the moment and to make the best of whatever Providence allowed. Reinforced by his contingent of Cimarrons, Drake decided to take the strongest eighteen of his men and attempt an overland expedition against the mule route to Spanish warehouses at Venta de Cruces on the upper Chagres River. Somewhere during that march, Drake gained his first glimpse of the Pacific Ocean. One can imagine Drake, exhausted and beyond frustration, offering a silent oath to sail those waters one day where he would take King Philip's gold at its very source. Drawing on the account of Drake's nephew entitled *Drake Revived*, Charles Sugden envisions what it must have been like for Drake to see what only a few Europeans had ever seen:

FRANCIS DRAKE   ECHOES OF THE DRAGON'S DRUM

"Another four days brought Drake to 'a very high hill, lying east and west, like a ridge', and upon its summit an enormous tree into which the cimarrones had cut steps that they might ascend to the top, where a viewing platform had been established. The captain accompanied Pedro to the bower to behold a sight few Englishmen had yet seen. Lying to the west in the clear light, across the treetops, was the mighty Pacific Ocean itself. Twisting round, Drake could see in the opposite direction the Caribbean that he knew so well. History and art have often dwelt upon this moment, sensing its significance and the inspiration with which it filled the English commander. Perhaps, with the benefit of hindsight, commentators have exaggerated the episode, but it was notable nonetheless. Drake saw a vision of the future here, the basis of another adventure. Just as he had led the corsairs to the isthmus highway, so he now grasped the possibility of unlocking the door to the Pacific, where none but the Spaniards and the occasional Portuguese had gone from Europe before, and which was still largely a mystery even to them. There and then Drake 'besought almighty God of his goodness to give him life and leave to sail once in an English ship in that sea.' And when he reached the ground John Oxenham, the Plymouth man who now stood as Drake's second-in-command, clambered up the tree to partake of the same exhilaration. A brave and respected man, but stern and grave, he seldom gave way to emotion, but now 'protested that unless our captain did beat him from his company he would follow him by God's grace.' Both men would fulfil their pledge to furrow the Pacific, but, while to one it would bring glory, to the other it would bring death."[35]

Ever the believer in the Providence of God, Francis Drake most assuredly

FRANCIS DRAKE   ECHOES OF THE DRAGON'S DRUM

proceeded from his experience of seeing the Pacific with renewed vigor. One failure piled upon another might have stymied a lesser man, but not this captain. His band of Englishmen and Cimarrons arrived at the mule train trail just before the gold and silver caravan and finally Providence appeared to favor his endeavor. But there was to be yet one more setback. While hiding in wait to attack the caravan, one of Drake's men gave away their position, and the Spanish fled leaving behind a few straggling mules loaded with trade goods. Still no gold or silver.

Using the captured mules as mounts the weary men made their way to Venta de Cruces where Drake's Cimarron allies vented rage in a bloody orgy of arson and looting. Returning to Fort Diego, Drake came upon the French Huguenot captain, Guillaume le Tetu. Now with yet another ally, Drake planned one last attempt at the overland treasure trail. On April 28, 1573, thirty-five sailors led by Drake and Tetu and accompanied by a large contingent of Cimarrons ambushed the mule train. After a brief but furious battle that left a number of French sailors either wounded or dead, the Spaniards fled leaving more gold and silver any could hope to transport back to England. Knowing the enemy was bound to rally quickly, Drake ordered his men to bury what treasure they could not move. Some of the wounded were beyond transporting and were left behind, including Tetu on whom the Spaniards took revenge in full measure. Once the Spanish left, Drake returned hoping to recover the wounded and buried silver. Tetu did not survive his torture, but there was a fair amount of silver plate. The French and English divided their plunder, and Francis Drake prepared to return to Plymouth.

On August 9, 1573 the *Pasha* and the ships captured during the

FRANCIS DRAKE — ECHOES OF THE DRAGON'S DRUM

expedition to the Spanish Main sailed into Plymouth's harbor. It was Sunday morning and most of the good people of Plymouth sat gathered where Francis Drake would surely have been if not at sea—in church. What records exist indicate that word began to filter through the congregation that the captain, his ships, and men had finally returned home. Nearly a year and a half had passed without word good or bad as to what had become of their men who went to sea.

The townspeople filtered down to the docks that Sunday morning to ships laden with treasure, glad reunions for some, and the resigned realization for many that both reward and penalty accompanied those who dare cross the Atlantic. More than half of Drake's men had fallen to sword, arrow, and disease and were buried in lands or waters that few of their family members would ever visit. However, those who did return brought riches for themselves and their families, riches of which most sailors could only dream. There existed few niches in the tight Elizabethan society where those who were neither royalty nor nobility nor gentry could escape the condition to which they were born in life, but these men had found just such a place.

Along with riches, Drake and his men returned with tales to be told around campfires, stoves, and alehouse tables time and again. At last, England could say it had tweaked King Philip and his sanctimonious New World overlords. By twisting "the tail of the Catholic king's mules" in their raids on the Isthmus of Panama, they had vicariously twisted the despised King of Spain's beard as well. With limited formal education and even less social standing, Francis Drake returned to his country at the age of 35 a financial success and a budding national hero. His first

Francis Drake — Echoes of the Dragon's Drum

forays into the Spanish Main gave him something no amount of plunder could. Other of Elizabeth's Sea Dogs such as Hawkins and Wynter were bothersome to Spain, but it was Drake that gained King Philip's attention. After all, it is hard to ignore a dragon once it spreads its wings and strikes at the heart of one's kingdom.

Rise to Importance Back at Home (1575)

*Imbath your Angel-feathers loftie quill
In fluent amber-dropping Castalie,
That liquid gold may from your pen distill,
Encarving characters of memorie,
In brasen-leav'd bookes of eternitie:
Be DRAKES worth royalized by your wits,
That DRAKES high name may coronize your writs.*

—Rev. Charles Fitzgeffrey

Over the next three years, the enterprising captain parlayed his gains into a successful merchant business. He purchased and built his own vessels, sending them off to distant ports under the command of dependable officers. Wealth could not buy the respect of peerage, but it could purchase connections. Drake's daring raids in Panama with his band of barely healthy Englishmen, French allies, and escaped slaves had the attention of the Queen's court and eventually Elizabeth herself. From the time he piloted his little barque in the English Channel until he returned with Spanish treasure, Francis Drake proved himself to be a man who got things done. Many in the royal court and among those that commanded in the navy were prone to excessive caution to the point of inaction, but not this young captain. Elizabeth needed such a

FRANCIS DRAKE   ECHOES OF THE DRAGON'S DRUM

man, but timing and politics dictated that it would be a few more years before the Queen could fully employ Drake's unique abilities.

Drake was now indeed rich and a hero to the mariners of the West Country, but he had stirred up havoc in the royal courts of both Spain and England. He had been off, under the authority of a royal marque, causing as much mischief as possible in the Spanish Main, but his return to Plymouth unfortunately coincided with better relations between Elizabeth and Philip. This would not be the last time the ever-advancing Drake found himself throttled by his ever-cautious Queen. Sugden explains:

> "In the Netherlands the Duke of Alba now had a full-scale insurrection on his hands, and he doubted that he could restore obedience while Elizabeth remained unfriendly and the English Channel was effectively closed to Spanish shipping. Nor was Alba alone in wishing an end to his damaging dispute with England. About the queen herself there was, it is true, a bellicose cabal of councillors headed by the Joint Principal Secretary, Francis Walsingham, who urged greater English intervention on the part of embattled Protestants in France and the Netherlands. But Elizabeth had burned her fingers in foreign adventures before, and instinctively shrank from extreme measures. Unofficially, she permitted her subjects to assist the Huguenots, but she would not commit herself any further to their cause. Spain and England did the sensible thing, and came to terms. Both agreed not to harbour aliens unfriendly to the other, and Philip promised to afford the Netherlands greater liberties and to prevent the Inquisition further molesting English sailors. For her part, Elizabeth undertook to settle

FRANCIS DRAKE — ECHOES OF THE DRAGON'S DRUM

the matter of her seizure of the Spanish ships and to discourage her seamen from raiding Philip's commerce as pirates or privateers. The arrival of the most dangerous of her corsairs at such a time was, to say the least, impolitic. It appears that, soon after his return, Drake was advised to keep a low profile and that he was at sea and out of harm's way until the convention of Bristol had successfully restored a degree of amity between Spain and England in 1574."[36]

One of the realities of naval enterprises of Drake's day was the speed, or lack thereof, at which communication traveled. During Drake's year and four months of doing the Queen's tacit bidding, she had mended fences with Spain and now made sure to keep her Sea Dogs in check, forbidding the seizure and plundering of Spanish ships. As a result, Drake wisely kept a low profile after returning from the New World. He was so quiet that little is known about his enterprises during the first two years following his hero's welcome home.

Drake's next appearance on the scene involved an issue that, though local, was connected to Spain and thus of supreme interest to him. Ireland was a troubled land, fiercely independent and once again a concern to mother England. This time it proved itself bothersome on two fronts: one strategically and the other religious. Ireland lay to the vulnerable west of England and served to protect that front from both Spanish and French invasion. Should it be overrun by invaders or ally with them, England would be fully exposed.

Except for a small minority of its population, Ireland remained a Gaelic society. It ruled itself by Gaelic rules of succession, law, and

FRANCIS DRAKE — ECHOES OF THE DRAGON'S DRUM

land ownership. Its people consisted predominantly of a peasantry that maintained its way of life by raising and bartering livestock and produce. Irish land owning freeholders recognized a ruling family that wasn't Tudor, and even the Irish of English descent adhered to Gaelic traditions. This meant that Ireland was a political and social wildcard always threatening to destabilize Elizabeth's drive to empire. And Ireland was resolutely Roman Catholic and therefore a haven for the counter-reformers eager to return England to Roman Catholic rule.

King Henry VIII declared Ireland under the rule of the English Crown and thus endeavored to convince the Irish chiefs to receive English title to the land they already controlled. His one stipulation required they introduce English law and religion and pledge fealty to the king. But the Irish were a stubborn lot, and the "surrender and regrant" policy of Henry helped little in bringing Ireland under English rule. "To the Elizabethans a combination of confiscation, colonization and plantation seemed an answer to the Irish problem. The lands of recalcitrant Irish would be seized and assigned to English adventurers, who undertook to settle the land with immigrants from England, grant them title, and develop in Ireland loyal communities which might support the English army against the Irish in times of difficulty."[37]

The policy itself became a never-ending source of animosity and conflict. Near and outright rebellion hung as a perpetual cloud that threatened to rain down trouble on Elizabeth in a time when the last thing she needed was another theater of battle. To her east, Spain held a death grip on the Netherlands, and she would not allow the same thing to happen to her west. Elizabeth's determination to quell the problem she

FRANCIS DRAKE — ECHOES OF THE DRAGON'S DRUM

inherited from her father remained with her throughout her forty-four years on the throne. Since the Sea Dogs comprised a major component in England's navy, it is not surprising that Raleigh and Drake appear as players in Elizabeth's move to put down rebellion in that land.

Like so much else of what she did, the Queen chose private enterprise to deal with the Ireland problem. Mariners of the west country of England were naturals to provide ships and sailors to quell rebellion in nearby Ireland, and thus Francis Drake captained a ship that transported men and supplies. It is almost certain than Drake had no idea or approved of what happened when those troops left his ship, because he was commanded to anchor off shore. Even so, what occurred inland remains a dark stain on supposedly genteel merry old England. Over the next two days, as Drake and his men killed time off shore, the English rooted out and slaughtered over 600 men, women, and children. Since few biographers have cared to cover this period in Drake's life, one has to turn again to Sugden for comment: "It must be assumed that Drake neither approved of nor participated in the massacre at Rathlin. He probably assisted the besiegers in landing men, stores and guns at the beginning of the operation, and thereafter cruised off shore to ensure that no help reached the island. The frigates were apparently busy, for they captured and burned eleven Scottish galleys. Time would show that Drake had the capacity for ruthlessness of a kind, but he was not an inhumane man, and he had already shown in his raids in the West Indies that he would attempt to deal with prisoners as generously as circumstances permitted. He had never killed unresisting Spaniards nor prisoners, and he had protected them from the cimarrones. And Norris's murder of the Scots of Rathlin was not only not Drake's way; it was not his war. If he found the humanity to protect the hated Spaniards, whom he held responsible for the débâcle at San Juan d'Ulua, we cannot suppose he was the man to condone the murder of Scottish or Irish people against whom he bore no grudges."[38]

This did not make for the best chapter in Francis Drake's life, but nevertheless it does not paint him as an evil man. Incidents of slaughtering innocents were so common in that day that only a handful of historians and biographers even bothered to chronicle the Irish rebellion of 1574. The storm clouds of Spanish conquest always loomed on the horizon blotting out concern for anything deemed of lesser importance. Perhaps Drake later learned of the massacre, but it is more likely he did not. For now he enjoyed a wife he spent far more time away from than with, managed his growing businesses, and nurtured his burgeoning influence with the Queen.

While these quiet years may seem a waste for one so adventurous and bold as Francis Drake, what he busied himself with during this period of his life proved essential to any future plans he might have. Though he returned with enough wealth to purchase an estate and firmly establish himself in business, Drake was still of modest means in comparison to those who financed well-furbished fleets. Just as Columbus learned barely seventy-five years earlier, patronage mattered even more than vision. And a well-manned multi-ship expedition could not happen without state backing. Ever since he climbed that tree in Panama and spied the Pacific Ocean, Drake had dreamed of returning to take Englishmen where only Spaniards had gone before. It was time to put his knack for cultivating patronage to work.

Part IV

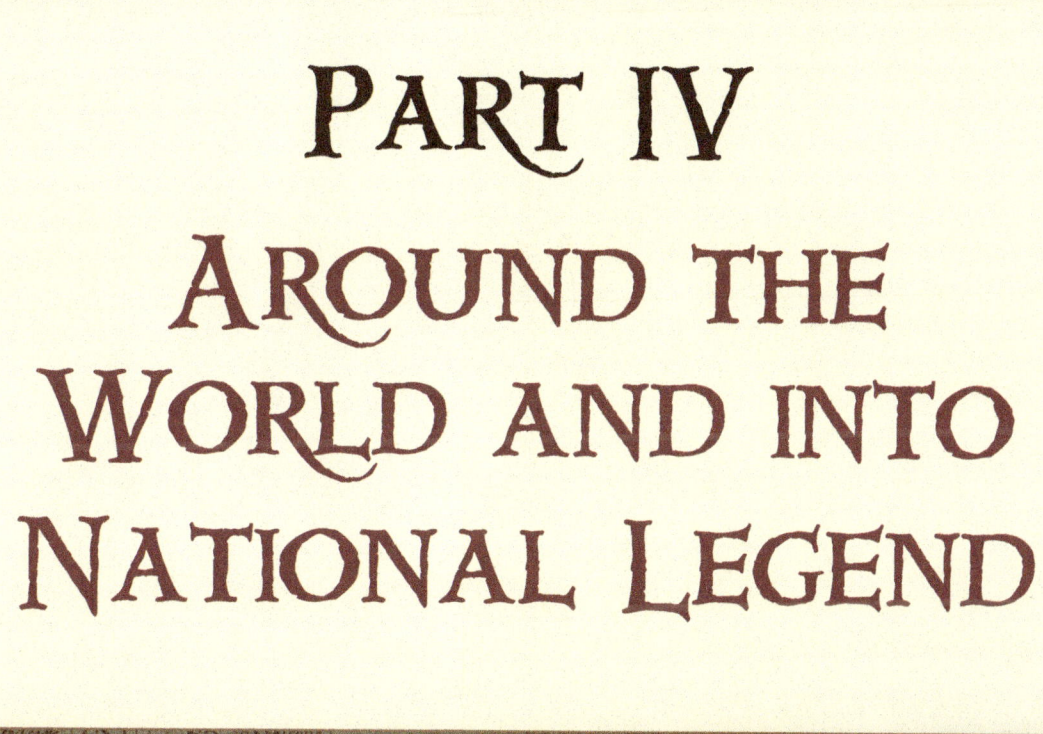

Around the World and into National Legend

M. DE L'ACADEMIE ROYALE des SCIENCES
et quelques autres et sur les memoires les plus recens
PAR M. DE L'ISLE

FRANCIS DRAKE   ECHOES OF THE DRAGON'S DRUM

Nor can it be in vain that Francis Drake,
Your noble hero, recently sailed round
The vast circumference of Earth (a feat Denied to man by many centuries),
To show how Father Neptune circumscribes
The continents, and wanders in between
To keep two worlds apart.

—Sir Humphrey Gilbert, 1582

"In January 1578, near the coast in northern Chile, a merchant snoozing in the shade of a tree woke from his siesta to find himself surrounded by a group of armed men. They seemed to be in high good humour, and were passing around 13 bars of silver taken from the saddlebags on his mule. They looked like Spanish soldiers, wearing the familiar morions on their heads and thickly padded doublets, but they spoke a language he did not understand.

"Their leader, a stocky man with piercing eyes set in a round head with reddish-brown curly hair, a light red moustache and a pointed beard, asked by gestures where the silver came from. The merchant replied that it came from the silver mine at Huantajaya. The strange men tried but could not pronounce the word. 'Want-a-what-ah?' asked one of them, and the rest fell about laughing.

"After they departed, taking his worldly wealth with them, the merchant hurried back to the town of Tarapacá, where he reported the theft to the authorities. Not long afterwards a bonded drover arrived to report an

FRANCIS DRAKE ECHOES OF THE DRAGON'S DRUM

ambush by the same group of strangers, not far from the town. They had stolen his team of eight llamas, each loaded with 100 pounds' weight of refined silver from the Huantajaya mine, enough to coin 12,800 pesos (pieces of eight) worth about £ 2,910 (equivalent to some £ 436,500 in 2010).

"Later a pinnace arrived from Valparaíso, far to the south, to report that a heavily armed ship manned by uncouth foreigners had raided the main port of Chile. They had stolen several tons of wine from storehouses and had broken into more of the same on a ship in the harbour. Pausing only to get drunk, the foreigners looted the ship of everything portable, including a quantity of refined gold from the mines at Valdivia, further south at the fighting frontier with the fierce Araucano Indians.

"Worst of all, they profaned a crucifix made of gold and emeralds, tearing the golden figure of Our Lord from it. All agreed these outrages could only be the work of the dreaded luteranos franceses, the French Protestant enemies of God and Spain who had been raiding the American dominions of His Catholic Majesty King Felipe II for many decades.

"Only later did they learn from Perú, where the foreigners raided the port of Callao before capturing a treasure ship on the high seas, that they had proudly identified themselves as ingleses, Englishmen, and that their stocky, curly-haired leader went by the fearsome name of el Draque—the Dragon."[39]

Though involving a small percentage of his storied life, Francis Drake's circumnavigation of the globe rightly deserves the longest chapter in

FRANCIS DRAKE   ECHOES OF THE DRAGON'S DRUM

any chronicle of his adventures. No one event, not even the famed battle with the Spanish Armada a few years to come, more demonstrates the kind of man Drake was and why England so needed him at this particular time in history. Francis Drake was no statesman or political negotiator. Francis Walsingham, the Joint Principal Secretary of State, was the former and Queen Elizabeth the latter, but this voyage would make Drake a leader of a different sort. The nation needed a hero. It needed Drake. The Dragon now prepared to carry England to a place and stature in the world it had not known before.

M. DE L'ACADEMIE ROYALE des SCIENCES
et quelques autres et sur les memoires les plus recens
PAR M. DE L'ISLE

FRANCIS DRAKE — ECHOES OF THE DRAGON'S DRUM

Turning the Dream into Reality (1577)

And in your fighting evermore, think you are Englishmen,
Then every one of you I hope will slay of Spaniards ten,
Or any else whatever they be, that shall disturb your peace
And seek by any kind of mean your quiet to decease.

—Henry Roberts, *A Most Friendly Farewell*

For many months Drake engaged himself in sending letters to men high in the court and government to plant in their minds and imaginations what was already full-blown in his. Though often characterized as impatient and merely lucky, Drake now navigated the waters of politics, custom, and religion with a resolute patience. It was a different kind of adventure for Drake. Rather than face Conquistador swords, native arrows, and treacherous waters, he now waded carefully through the waters of etiquette and personage. In his own abbreviated account of this quest for patronage to finance his expedition, Drake writes of how he carried a letter of introduction from the Earl of Essex to Francis Walsingham, the Joint Principal Secretary of State.

The two Francises were a perfect match in their distrust for and determination to circumvent the Spanish. Walsingham had already established, at his own expense, an elaborate and effective network of spies with one objective in mind—to detect and foil foreign plots

FRANCIS DRAKE — ECHOES OF THE DRAGON'S DRUM

against Elizabeth. While ambassador in Paris, he narrowly escaped the St. Bartholomew's Eve massacre of Protestants, which cemented his distrust of any nation dominated by Roman Catholic influence. He was one of a few in the Queen's inner circle convinced that war with Spain was not only possible but inevitable. Along with Robert Dudley, the Earl of Leicester, Walsingham advocated a stronger navy and more aggressive measures against King Philip. Neither Spain nor England could field an army or man a navy without substantial capital, and the obvious source of such capital now lay in the Americas. Philip had taken the Netherlands, absorbed Portugal, and barely disguised his intentions for England. His treasure fleets ensured he could take whatever else he wanted. Walsingham understood, as did Drake, that the key to weakening Spain was not in Europe, but rather at the source from which it filled its coffers, the New World.

As Drake tells it, what caught Walsingham's attention was Drake's claim that his own expertise might be valuable in an enterprise against Spain. Anything that was of value in slowing Spain interested Walsingham, so he immediately sent for Drake. When Drake arrived, Walsingham spread a map before him and asked how Philip could best be irritated in repayment for the trouble the Spanish king had caused Elizabeth. Drake pointed to a place on the map, but resolutely told Walsingham that he would not sign his name to any such plan, because, "If it should please God to take Her Majesty away it might be that some prince might reign that might be in league with the King of Spain, and then will my own hand be a witness against myself."[40] The area on the map Drake pointed to was the Pacific. If Spain had an achilles heel, he proclaimed, it was in the west. Spain viewed the ocean Drake saw from high in that tree a

FRANCIS DRAKE — ECHOES OF THE DRAGON'S DRUM

few years earlier as its private property. Drawing from his experience in raiding the mule trains of Panama, Francis Drake assured Walsingham that though the Spanish seem invincible in their own backyard, across the Atlantic, their arrogance and self-confidence made their treasure fleets a soft target. Patience had brought Drake before the right man in the Queen's court, but now his ability to motivate and press an agenda sealed the deal. Francis Drake promised that, if he were given what he needed, England would no longer have to accept second and third place in the race for the riches of the Americas.

Now all that was needed was the money to finance the expedition. Initial investors included Drake (£1,000), Sir William Winter (£750), John Hawkins (£500), and a few other close associates. From there Drake proceeded to gather around his project a small band of influential patrons: the Earl of Lincoln, Christopher Hatton, the Earl of Leicester, and Walsingham himself. The syndicate backing Drake thus represented the navy and the court, but far less the merchants. This is significant because, while disguised as a trading expedition, Drake had no intention of being a floating shopkeeper. His intent and determination was to follow the path of Magellan and round South America for the Pacific.

After a great deal of surreptitious maneuvering and delays, Francis Drake at last had his audience with the Queen. "[I] came not to Her Majesty," said Drake, "that night for that it was too late. But the next day coming to her presence, these or the like words she said: "Drake! So it is that I would gladly be revenged on the King of Spain for diverse injuries that I have received." And [she] said further that I was the only man who might do this exploit, and withal craved my advice therein;

FRANCIS DRAKE ECHOES OF THE DRAGON'S DRUM

who told Her Majesty of the small good that was to be done in Spain but the only way was to annoy him by the Indies."[41] During that brief conversation Elizabeth stressed the necessity that such a mission be clandestine in nature. Few in London were to be trusted, for Philip had spies everywhere.

Elizabeth's caution was well warranted. As long as Mary Stuart (Mary, Queen of Scots) lived, she had her own loyal supporters. In addition, the Inquisition harassed the crews of English ships trading in Spanish ports, and Philip refused to grant reasonable terms to his Protestant subjects in the Netherlands. A special ambassador had been sent to Madrid in an effort to resolve such issues, but he had returned empty-handed. Elizabeth began to seriously consider recognizing the sovereignty of the Netherlands, as Philip's rebel provinces were asking. Tensions continued to mount as the Privy Council debated steps against Spain and acceptance of the Dutch proposal. In March 1576, Elizabeth summoned Parliament to provide for the defense of the realm. That spring offered a perfect political atmosphere for the mission Francis Drake had in mind.

What might surprise many today is that Francis Drake did not look to make a trip around the world at all. Matching Magellan's feat or setting some record was not his goal, for he was too much a pragmatist for that. In truth, Drake had his sights set on something that had long been thought possible by a number of explorers in England. He was hoping to circumnavigate the Americas. For years, Englishmen looked for a Northwest Passage they believed could carry them across the northern part of America to India. Such a passage, Drake reasoned, would offer

FRANCIS DRAKE   ECHOES OF THE DRAGON'S DRUM

a way to come behind the Spanish and intercept their treasure fleet in the Pacific.

Bawkf explains: "The only other means of confirming the existence of the strait was to send an expedition southward, all the way around South America, or Africa and Asia, and onward into the North Pacific to look for its outlet, and this became the key that unlocked Drake's project. In consideration for being permitted to pass through Magellan's Strait to raid Spanish shipping, Drake undertook to continue northward and search for the Strait of Anian. If successful, he would attempt to return to England through the northwest passage, completing a circumnavigation of America."[42]

If he succeeded, Francis Drake believed he would deal a decisive blow to Spain. This was stuff of which modern espionage movies are made. No Tom Clancy or Robert Ludlum novel can match the intrigue, secrecy, daring, and outright audaciousness of the mission. It was "the most daring naval expedition and the most ambitious voyage ever conceived."[43] Of Drake's many adventures, none better encapsulates the daring, tenacity, and determined loyalty of Drake than his famous voyage where no other Englishman had ever gone, the ends of the earth.

On July 9, 1577, Francis Drake wrote to the government and claimed his approved royal bounty for construction of his new bark: "The same Frances hath of late caused to be erected made and builded at his own expenses proper cost and charge one ship or vessel called the Pelican of Plymouth of the burden of one hundred and fifty tonnes."[44] A bounty was a bill paid by the Crown to private ship owners, who then

FRANCIS DRAKE ECHOES OF THE DRAGON'S DRUM

constructed armed ships with the understanding they could be called upon for the defense of the realm whenever needed. The result was a ship that belonged to Drake to do with as he pleased unless the Queen required otherwise.

The ship Drake built, christened the *Pelican*, was small even by the standards of his day. Stem to stern it was barley 100 feet in length and, at best, perhaps 21 feet in beam. This meant that a shallow draft vessel barely larger than the area of a modern-day tennis court was intended to transport Drake, his men, and provisions across thousands of miles of the Atlantic and then through the notoriously treacherous Straits of Magellan into the Pacific. By design, Drake intended his new ship to appear both to outside observer and crew alike as nothing more than a three-mated bark, a typical merchant vessel. Like everything else about this mission, appearances were deceiving. From the day Drake pointed to a map with instructions to make no record of his observations until long after the *Pelican* and the rest of his little fleet were far at sea, Francis Drake intended to carry out a classic covert mission. The Queen had plausible deniability, and he had a green light to attempt a voyage that would ensure his place in the history books. It did not take long, once they were out to sea, for the crew to realize the *Pelican* was no ordinary merchant ship.

Her hold was large enough to carry four prefabricated pinnaces along with supplies and provisions. The special double-planked oak-timbered hull was strong enough to endure the stresses of the long voyage. Drawing only 13 feet of water, the *Pelican* could navigate shallow coastal waters, something Spain's galleons could not do. With a mainmast rising 90 feet, double canvas sails, and specially designed topgallants, this ship could make the most of the lightest winds and outrun just about anything it might face. Samuel Bawlf notes that the *Pelican* was deceptively well-armed: "Appearances aside, the *Pelican* was also much better armed than any merchantman. Above her hold, her gundeck, having about five feet of headroom, carried fourteen cannons mounted to fire from seven gunports on each side of the ship. The cannons were slender, long-range demi-culverins, each weighing about 3,400 pounds and capable of hurling a 9K-pound ball at an enemy well before it could come close enough to reply with its own guns. In addition, there were four more of these mounted above deck to fire from her bow and stern, together with several smaller, breech-loading guns known as falconets. Altogether, the weight of the *Pelican*'s ordinance alone was more than thirty tons. She also carried a variety of incendiary devices that could be launched at the sails and rigging of an adversary to set them afire; and her armory contained ample numbers of harquebuses, crossbows, pikes, longbows, shields, helmets, corselets, swords, and pistols to equip her crew for a fight at sea or on land."[45]

In the months leading up to Drake's expedition, international political tensions approached the boiling point. Tensions between England and Spain, always present, were more pronounced than ever. In 1576, Dutch Catholics and Protestants had united under the leadership of William of Orange, elected their own assembly, and joined to fight for independence from Spain. Philip responded by appointing his half-brother, Don John of Austria, to put down the rebellion. Then in the early months of 1577 Walsingham's spies steadily exposed a plot by Don John and the Duke of Guise to invade England with 10,000 men, depose Elizabeth, and install Mary Stuart on the throne. Don John planned to wed Mary and rule England jointly with her. Walsingham's evidence of the scheme infuriated Elizabeth. This report removed whatever hesitations the Queen harbored before and ensured Francis Drake clear passage to move forward with his plans.

In late June of 1578, John Hawkins drafted a fictitious plan to the effect that Drake was embarking on a trading voyage to Alexandria. Spies were everywhere in the Queen's court and the news of a trading voyage didn't salve their suspicions of what the Queen and her Sea Dog were up to. A month later, Philip's representative in London, Antonio de Guaras, received a dispatch from one of his spies, warning: "Francis Drake is going to the Antilles, although they are spreading the rumour that they are going to Tripoli . . . there is no doubt they are going where I say, and they will do much harm if your mercy does not take measures to keep them from going."[46] Always one step ahead in the espionage game, Walsingham managed to field more disinformation that led de Guaras to advise King Philip that Drake's actual mission was to the Prince of Scotland.

What Drake did during this season of misinformation and political jockeying is uncertain. Drake's meager memoirs do however give us one snippet of a conversation he had with Queen Elizabeth before he returned to Plymouth. During that farewell meeting Elizabeth presented him with a sea cap on which was embroidered, "The Lord guide and preserve thee until the end." She also gave him one of her swords, and then said, "We do account that he which striketh at thee, Drake, striketh at us."[47]

From England to South America (1578)

Sir Drake, whom well the world's end knows,
Which thou didst compass round,
And whom both pole of heaven once saw
Which North and South do bound.
The stars above will make thee known,
If men here silent were,
The Sun himself cannot forget
His fellow Traveler.

—Anonymous

Neither Drake nor those in his inner circle who understood the true nature of this mission held any illusion that it would be without trials. Even the most seasoned sailors would have second thoughts about signing up for such a mission if they but knew. It was incredibly daring for a number of reasons: capture meant certain death at the hands of the Spanish; they would have to secure much of their needed provisions during the voyage by whatever means necessary; and, finally, the only way to the Pacific was by way of the treacherous southern tip of South America.

The voyage did not begin well. Some historians have mused that perhaps Drake risked setting sail in the notoriously fickle winter English seas because he did not want to give Elizabeth a chance to change her mind

FRANCIS DRAKE — ECHOES OF THE DRAGON'S DRUM

and scuttle the voyage. If so, it would not be the first or last time that Elizabeth, ever moving pieces on the game board of European politics, did such a thing. Whatever the reason, Drake departed during the early winter in November of 1577, but the rough seas soon forced him to return to land and dock at the port of Falmouth in Cornwall. Undaunted by the temporary setback, Drake sailed again on December 13th. The 165 souls that sailed from England that day included captains, crewmen, gentlemen-adventurers, special artificers, trained surveyors, musicians, boys, and Drake's page, Jack Drake.

Drake's plan all along involved conscripting ships and stores as needed. The five little ships were severely overcrowded, so Drake quickly purchased the *Santa Maria*, captured by its captain off the coast of Africa. During the first leg of their journey, Drake continued to capture and conscript vessels as opportunity arose until his fleet had more than doubled in size. Aboard the English ships, the gentlemen and more than one captain complained that the expedition was deteriorating into petty piracy, but Drake had good reason for seizing so many vessels: the fleet was carrying only a portion of the provisions needed on its long voyage, and had to avail itself of every occasion to supplement those provisions en route. Even in these acts of confiscation, Drake showed himself different from many of the Spanish Conquistadors and the infamous pirates of the next century. As soon as his original fleet had provision enough to continue, he released the captured ships and their crews. Francis Drake did not want to rob and plunder Portuguese fishermen and traders, but saw them as a means to an end—getting at the Spanish.

FRANCIS DRAKE   ECHOES OF THE DRAGON'S DRUM

The *Santa Maria* remained with the fleet as Drake had purchased the ship and retained its captain, Nuño da Silva. A 100 ton trader, the *Santa Maria* was loaded down with linen, cloth, canvas, tools, and implements, all of which Drake planned to put to good use. Just as important, the holds were packed with casks of wine and enough water for the rest of the voyage. But it was the ship's captain that interested Drake the most. Nuño da Silva was a veteran of the waters Drake intended to sail and of which he knew little. Equally important, the captain had charts needed for the voyage, including soundings for that coast as far south as the Río de la Plata. Removing da Silva to the *Pelican*, Drake promised fair compensation for the loss of his ship. Fletcher, the expedition chaplain, recorded that when da Silva heard they were bound for the South Sea, he was more than eager to accompany them. It is obvious from this that Drake's crew was by now fully aware of where they were headed.

Overcrowding proved no problem for long as many of the crew perished in the Atlantic. So many died at sea that by the time Drake reached San Julian off present day Argentina, he did not have enough in his crew to effectively man all the ships. As a result, he made the hard decision to leave the *Swan* and the *Christopher* on the coast. The newly acquired *Mary* showed itself to have a rotting hulk, making it no longer seaworthy, and so it was burned. Drake and his crew made land in San Julian to discover a grim reminder of how dangerous what they were attempting could be. There to greet them on the sandy shore was a welcoming committee of bleached skeletons. Just 50 years earlier, the men who now stared at them from sightless sockets had dared mutiny during Magellan's voyage around the world. To remind other sailors to think better before daring to question their captain, Magellan had them

FRANCIS DRAKE — ECHOES OF THE DRAGON'S DRUM

killed and left their unburied bodies hung up for all who followed to see. Drake could not have planned a better object lesson for any who might consider turning back.

Modern sensibilities might be appalled at such things, but this kind of law was more than necessary on the seas. It is hard for a modern reader to comprehend what Francis Drake faced with each voyage he commanded. 16th century mariners faced a host of obstacles to a successful voyage. Sickness claimed far more seamen than sword or cannon, and food and water were always an issue, but the one cloud that always hung over a ship's captain was mutiny. Once Francis Drake and his ships left Plymouth, the only law was the captain and the only deterrents to breaking that law were the strength of his character and the force of his will.

Because of these realities, strict maritime laws had already been codified by the time Drake and his men stared at Magellan's silent reminders. Fowler lists a few of these laws understood by every seaman before he stepped on a ship:

> "Orders to be Used in the King's Majesty's Navy by the Sea"
>
> "If any man kill another within the ship, he that doeth the deed shall be bound quick to the dead man, and so be cast into the sea, and a piece of ordnance shot off after they be thrown into the sea.
>
> "If any man draw a weapon within the ship to strike his captain, he shall lose his right hand.
>
> "If any man within the ship draws any weapon or causeth tumult or

FRANCIS DRAKE   ECHOES OF THE DRAGON'S DRUM

likelihood of murder or bloodshed within the ship, he shall lose his right hand as is aforesaid.

"If any man within the ship steal or pick money or clothes within the ship duly proved, he shall be three times dipped at the bowsprit and dipped down two fathoms within the water, and kept alive, and at the next shore towed aland bound the boat's stern, with a loaf of bread and a can of beer, and banished from the King's ship forever.

"If any man within the ship do sleep his watch three times and so proved, this be his punishment: the first time he shall be headed at the main mast with a bucket of water poured on his head. The second time he shall be armed, his hands hailed up by a rope, and two buckets of water poured into his sleeves. The third time he should be bound in the main mast with certain gun chambers tied to his arms and as much pain to his body as the captain will. The fourth time and last punishment, being taken asleep he shall be hanged on the bowsprit end of the ship in a basket, with a can of beer, a loaf of bread, and a sharp knife, choose to hang there till he starve himself or cut himself into the sea."[48]

Ironically, it would not be long before Drake was faced with insurrection and possible mutiny from someone he personally enlisted for the voyage. During the time the fleet was temporarily delayed from leaving Plymouth, Drake dismissed James Styde, a provisioner. A few days after that, he called the gentlemen and some of the sailors together at his house in Plymouth with the intention of promoting a spirit of unity in the two very different groups of men. Later the same night, Thomas Doughty complained to one of the mariners that he should have been consulted

FRANCIS DRAKE   ECHOES OF THE DRAGON'S DRUM

before Drake dismissed Styde since, as claimed, he "shared command" of the expedition. Whether Doughty had been misled by others in the Queen's court to believe he indeed shared command or simply allowed misplaced ambitions to cloud his judgment remains a mystery. What is certain is that Doughty continued to foster doubt in the minds of others from the moment the voyage began until matters came to a head in South America. Distrust and dissension are greatly magnified in the closed confines of a vessel hardly the size of a tennis court in the middle of thousands of square miles of water. As a result, Doughty's words in Plymouth successfully sowed the first seeds of Drake's sailors' discontent. As the voyage got under way, things quieted down, but the matter was not settled. Doughty's antics were far from over.

A number of incidents foreshadowed what was to come before Drake and his crew found Magellan's not-so-merry men. In February, two months into the voyage, the *Santa Maria* was no longer needed. Drake ordered food and drink be ferried to the ship so da Silva could be on his way. According to Fletcher, Drake's trumpeter John Brewer and Edward Bright returned from the *Santa Maria* complaining that Thomas Doughty was pilfering from the ship. John Cooke, a Doughty sympathizer, disputed that story later, claiming that Doughty said it was actually Drake's brother Thomas that had done the stealing.

Bawlf writes of the incident: "Fletcher later wrote that Drake dismissed the matter as trivial but 'in discretion' sent Doughty to the *Pelican* while he remained on the *Santa Maria*. According to John Cooke, however, Drake flew into a rage and with 'great oaths' charged Doughty with falsely accusing his brother in order to undermine his own credibility as

FRANCIS DRAKE   ECHOES OF THE DRAGON'S DRUM

Captain-General, and 'swore by God's life' that he would not suffer it. However, Cooke said, 'Master Doughty's very friend,' Leonard Vicary, then intervened on his behalf, appealing for Drake to overlook the incident, 'which in the end he yielded unto and, to the outward show, forgave and seemed to forget all that had passed.'"[49]

Oddly enough, after the incident, Drake ordered Doughty to take nominal command of the *Pelican*. Some have conjectured that Drake might have done this to observe how Doughty would lead once the matter was resolved. That did not require long as the moment Doughty made deck on the *Pelican*, he ordered the men assembled and gave a speech, which began:

> *"My masters, the cause why I call you together is for that I have somewhat to say unto you from the General. The matter is this, that whereas there hath been great travails, fallings out, and quarrels among you and that every one of you have been uncertain whom to obey...therefore hath the General by his wisdom and discretion, set down order that all things might be better done with peace and quietness.*
>
> *"And for that he hath a special care of this place, being his admiral and chief ship...he hath sent me as his friend whom he trusteth to take charge in his place, giving unto me the special commandment to signify unto you that all matters by-past are forgiven and forgotten; upon this condition, that we have no more of your evil dealing hereafter.*
>
> *"And for the safer accomplishing hereof I am to tell you, that you are to obey one master in the absence of your General, who is to direct you in your business as touching navigation, which is Mr. Cuttill, whom you*

know to be a sufficient man."[50]

Up to this point in the speech, Doughty words remained consistent with that of a commander of a ship, but he was not finished. With his men's full attention, Doughty continued: "And for other matters, as the General has his authority from her highness the Queen's majesty and her Council such as hath not been committed almost to any subject afore this time—to punish at his discretion with death or other ways offenders; so he hath committed the same authority to me in his absence to execute upon those which are malefactors."[51]

Doughty had once again overstepped his bounds. Chaplain Fletcher later noted in his journal that Doughty was taking on himself "too great of a command." Others later complained as well to Drake that Thomas Doughty was overstepping his bounds, but for now Drake let the matter slide.

With the Doughty matter temporarily set aside, the fleet made slow headway for South America. As they approached the equator, progress became excruciatingly slow. By February 10, the ships sat motionless, caught in the doldrums of still, humid air under a blistering sun. After a series of brief, fitful starts followed by more days without wind to fill their sails, the ships finally found a steady wind and set their course southwest toward Brazil.

As the fleet approached Brazil, Drake remained aboard Nuño da Silva's ship, renamed the *Mary*, and joined his brother Thomas and the Portuguese captain to plot their course. Back aboard the *Pelican* Drake's hopes that Doughty might stay in check proved misplaced. Bawlf writes

FRANCIS DRAKE   ECHOES OF THE DRAGON'S DRUM

of the incident:

"Aboard the Pelican Thomas Doughty's antics continued. Approaching Master Cuttill and some of the mariners individually, he promised they would be rewarded if they did his bidding, and that he would use his influence to square whatever they did with the Queen and her council when they got back to England. It appears that Doughty's aim was to break away from Drake. At the same time Doughty's younger brother John allegedly boasted that the two of them possessed powers of witchcraft, claiming that they could call up the Devil in the form of a lion or bear, or poison their enemies by supernatural means. If the younger Doughty did make such claims, he was inviting serious trouble, because the Elizabethans commonly believed in and feared witchcraft, and nowhere was that dread more acute than among a group of superstitious sailors.

"Finally, in mid-ocean, the situation came to a head when Drake sent his trumpeter, John Brewer, over to the Pelican on an errand. As Brewer stepped aboard the Pelican, Thomas Doughty had him seized, bent over a barrel, and under the pretext of an amusement invited the assembled crew to join him in delivering a 'cobbey'—a rough spanking to Brewer's naked buttocks. When Drake learned of this humiliating treatment of his messenger, he sent some men to fetch Doughty. The religious service was under way when they returned with him, and Drake was reading from the Bible.

"As Doughty reached to climb aboard the Mary, Drake turned abruptly and shouted 'stay there Thomas Doughty, for I must send you to another

FRANCIS DRAKE   ECHOES OF THE DRAGON'S DRUM

place,' and then ordered that he be taken to the provision ship Swan and placed in the charge of Captain John Chester. Fletcher recorded that Doughty was removed 'in utter disgrace.'"[52]

At one point, as troubles approached the boiling point, Doughty had bragged to anyone who would listen aboard the *Swan* that Drake owed his advancement to him. Discussion later that same day turned to the growing discontent that Doughty's ramblings had encouraged. John Saracold, a seaman, brusquely observed that "if there were traitors aboard, Drake should deal with them as Magellan had done, and hang them as an example to others. Saracold did not name Doughty, but the gentleman he spoke with was plainly alarmed at the suggestion. 'Nay, softly!' he replied. 'His authority is none such as Magellan's was, for I know his authority so well as he himself does. And for hanging, it is for dogs, and not for

Francis Drake's Hat Stolen by Indians near Río de la Plata (Scene from Drake Expedition near Río de la Plata, Brazil, ca. 1578)

FRANCIS DRAKE   ECHOES OF THE DRAGON'S DRUM

men.'"[53]

The die had been cast for both Doughty and Drake. The tenuous relationship between seaman and gentlemen that existed on every such expedition now threatened to unravel, and such could not be allowed. Francis Drake knew he depended on the gentlemen and other investors for capital, but he depended on his seamen for his and their very lives. Even the hint of insurrection threatened more damage than any Spanish war ship, and it simply could not be tolerated. However, bad as such was, it may well have been Thomas Doughty's younger brother, John, who ensured the whole affair could only end one way. Superstitious sailors on many a voyage before had picked a Jonah from their crew when things went unexplainably wrong. Plagued with a succession of calms followed by violent storms, it did not take much for them to believe John Doughty was right about his brother's powers over evil forces. Drake needed nothing more to justify himself before his men or God for what must come next.

The problems with Thomas Doughty had been simmering for four months, the much-dreaded Magellan Strait and the frigid South Seas loomed close, and everyone needed a diversion. Relief showed itself with the appearance of natives who approached the sailor as they harbored to make repairs and replenish their provisions. The natives visited daily, growing more approachable the more they learned to trust the English. Drake's method of establishing rapport with the natives was the same used in more recent times by the Villas Boas brothers in their efforts to contact remote tribes of the Brazilian rainforest. The sailors left gifts on rods so that the Indians could approach them when

FRANCIS DRAKE — ECHOES OF THE DRAGON'S DRUM

they wished and leave their own offerings in trade. Gradually, relations formed between the two disparate people. "The native men proved to be ferocious-looking, though hardly the giants depicted in Spanish myth. They wore their hair long, painted themselves red, white and black, and if they went mostly naked they smeared their bodies with oil to keep out the cold. Bones or wood were thrust into their noses or lips. They fascinated the voyagers, who noted the Indians' love of music (especially the English trumpets and drums), their ability to produce a fire from two pieces of wood, their dances (in which, to the immense satisfaction of his men, Captain Winter participated) and their jollity. Amiable the Indians were, but the English also found them opportunistic thieves and one day as Drake was ashore an enterprising native snatched away his cap … and dashed away with it in triumph. The General understood the importance of good humor and patience in situations like this, and in the words of a mariner, Edward Cliffe, 'would suffer no man to hurt any of them.'"[54]

Strait of Magellan.

Francis Drake was a man of his times, yet somewhat beyond them. He did tolerate slavery early in his sailing days, and there is no record of him chastising his cousin John for continuing in the trade. However, he also never took or transported slaves again once he had his own ships. At every port of call, he displayed a

FRANCIS DRAKE ECHOES OF THE DRAGON'S DRUM

relative humanitarianism in the way he dealt with prisoners that set a precedent far above that of the French and the Spanish. When he came across the Cimarrons in Panama and learned what they had suffered at the hands of the Spanish, he cultivated their friendships and called them allies. As preparations continued for the assault on the Strait of Magellan, he displayed the same attitude of forbearance and friendship toward the South American Indians. Considering how the Spanish had treated these same people, they surely must have been grateful for Drake's appearance. Of course, Francis Drake did not believe their religion equal to his own. As a Christian, he believed the revelation of God in Scripture was absolute truth. However, Drake also possessed a sincere respect for peoples of other cultures that was absent from so many of the great explorers. Drake constantly spoke of the Cimarrons with affection. One of Drake's men later told a Spaniard, "those Negroes were the brothers of Captain Francis, who loved them dearly." And a Spanish prisoner of Drake's remarked that "he had heard Captain Francis say that he loved them, and that he spoke well of them, and every day he asked if they were in peace."[55] Unfortunately, few others shared Drake's attitude.

As often happened on such voyages, the ships in the fleet became separated, and weather and prevailing winds prevented Drake from backtracking to search for the now missing *Mary*. That ship along with Drake's brother and da Silva had not been seen for nearly two months. When Drake and his remaining ships anchored in a bay one hundred miles from Magellan's Strait, winds finally favored a renewed search for the *Mary*. Drake's ship and the *Mary* finally reunited on June 19. Thomas Drake and his crew had not touched land since leaving Rio de la Plata

FRANCIS DRAKE   ECHOES OF THE DRAGON'S DRUM

two months earlier. Their ship was intact but leaking profusely, the crew was exhausted, and many of the mariners were ill. Regrouping, Drake chose a bay in which to harbor his fleet, now down to just four ships. There they would sit out the winter before rounding South America.

Drake's ships passed the dismal gray cliffs of Port St. Julian on June 20, 1578 with every sailor and Gentleman fully aware of their history. As the crew stepped out on the beach, the gentle breeze that brushed across the sands whispered a story every sailor knew by heart. This was the place where, less than sixty years earlier, Spanish officers attempted a mutiny against their commander, Magellan, and paid the expected price when they failed. At least one officer's bleached bones still hung from a gibbet and two others had been swallowed up by the jungle where they had been left marooned. Perhaps the natives here still retained memories of Magellan and his cruel ways because their reception of Drake and his men was not nearly as welcoming as that of the first natives the Englishmen encountered. At least one officer was killed in the confrontation, and Drake and his men barely escaped disaster.

Even as they pressed on, ghosts of Magellan's mutiny followed them. Drake realized that Doughty now had a following of about thirty men, including a number of mariners who barely concealed their anxiety at being involved in such a hazardous adventure and welcomed any excuse to turn back for England. Even Captain Winter of the *Elizabeth*, although prudent in his remarks, was not enthusiastic about continuing the voyage. The potential for further discord in the company leading to bloodshed, mutiny, or desertion of one or more of the ships was therefore very real. Drake knew he could not bring charges of mutiny against Doughty

FRANCIS DRAKE — ECHOES OF THE DRAGON'S DRUM

without executing him. Even halfway around the world, politics and its intrigue remained close. Let Doughty live, and the mission was sure to fail. Put him to death and face uncertain repercussions at the journey's end. The whole Doughty affair was marked by a caution not common to Francis Drake. More often than not, his willingness to take chances brought him victory. However, this was a different kind of battle, one that favored name, prestige, and political connections above physical bravery. Something had to give, and at last Drake decided it would not be him.

On June 30 Drake assembled the entire company on shore and stood before them with Captain John Thomas at his side. He then called on Thomas to read statements taken from witnesses that had been privy to Doughty's mutinous talk throughout the voyage. Drake then called Doughty forward and said: "Thomas Doughty, you have here sought by diverse means, in as much as you may, to discredit me to the great hindrance and overthrow of this voyage, besides other great matters wherewith I have to charge you withal, the which if you can clear yourself of, you and I shall be very good friends, where to the contrary you have deserved death."

Upon Doughty's denial of the charges, Drake asked him how he wished to be tried. "Why, good General, let me live to come into my country, and I will there be tried by Her Majesty's laws," Doughty replied. "Nay, Thomas Doughty," Drake said, "I will here impanel a jury on you to inquire further of these matters that I have to charge you withal."[56]

At that point Doughty said he hoped Drake had a solid commission

FRANCIS DRAKE — ECHOES OF THE DRAGON'S DRUM

granting him the Queen's authority to make such a judgment. Apparently, Doughty knew Drake had no written commission from the Queen and counted on that fact to prevent his execution. Such was not to be the case. A jury of 40 mariners and gentlemen was chosen with Captain Winter as the foreman. After a brief exchange between Drake and Doughty, the time came for a verdict. Though the jury returned a verdict of guilty, it was left to the whole crew to decide Doughty's fate. The vote was nearly unanimous: Thomas Doughty must die.

The Golden Hinde galleon. Courtesy of Oxfordian Kissuth, Wikimedia Commons.

Two days later, on July 2, a most curious scene played out before the execution. Doughty requested to receive the sacrament from Chaplain Fletcher, and Drake asked to accompany him, "for the which Master Doughty gave hearty thanks, never once terming him other than 'my good captain.' Then Drake invited Doughty to dine with him in his tent, and they did so, "each cheering up the other and taking their leave by drinking to each other."[57] After the meal Doughty and Drake spoke privately before the accused was led away a few minutes later. With the entire crew as witness, Doughty knelt and prayed for the Queen and for the success of the voyage, and then asked forgiveness for himself and his allies. Then he placed his neck on the block and the ax fell ... along with all concerns of future mutiny.

On August 21, 1578 with the Strait of Magellan in sight, Drake held a ceremony in which he changed the name of his flagship from the *Pelican* to the *Golden Hind*. To the present day, the *Golden Hind* remains the most famous ship in all of British naval history.

All sailors believed the Strait of Magellan to be the only path from the Atlantic to the Pacific, and the few that dared its waters had paid a heavy price. Magellan's records estimated the route to be one hundred leagues, but beyond that offered few details. Maps of the area were woefully inaccurate, and Portuguese charts were vague. Bawlf vividly describes the Strait of Magellan:

> *"From the Atlantic, the strait squeezes through two narrows and then turns south and widens to about fifteen miles in Broad Reach. Initially the terrain on either side consists of low, rolling pampas, and Broad Reach afforded room for a square-rigged ship to maneuver in the face of a contrary wind. Still, there were hazards. The tides produce powerful currents, and the sea bottom is foul with jagged rocks. If a hemp anchor cable became snagged on one of these, it soon parted and the anchor was lost. Even if the ship was not driven ashore as a consequence, this was*

FRANCIS DRAKE ECHOES OF THE DRAGON'S DRUM

a serious mishap, for it was impractical to carry more than five or six anchors, and once they were gone a ship was helpless.

"Partway down Broad Reach the strait begins to cut through the tail of the rugged spine of South America—the Andes—and beyond this point the conditions rapidly worsen. Sudden, violent squalls hurl down the mountain slopes with such force that a sailing ship could be knocked over on its beam ends in seconds. At the southern end of Broad Reach numerous channels branch off, and the squalls often converge from several directions, churning up chaotic seas and tornado-like waterspouts.

"At Cape Froward the strait turns abruptly northwest and runs for 150 miles in a deep, narrow cut through the Andes before it reaches the Pacific, and it was here that sailors could be driven to despair. The currents created by the tides are swifter, the winds are even more boisterous, and for much of its length the channel is only two or three miles wide, leaving little room for a square-rigged ship to tack. Often for days or weeks on end powerful headwinds funnel down the strait from the Pacific. Moreover, the flanking cliffs and mountains plunge steeply into the sea, and the seabed falls away to great depths, so there were few places a ship could anchor. Then, when the wind finally lightened, an exhausted crew might claw their way to within sight of the open sea only to meet a fresh headwind and be forced back down the strait, possibly all the way back to Cape Froward before they could get into a sheltered anchorage."[58]

Most of what is known about Drake's voyage through the 343 miles of

FRANCIS DRAKE ECHOES OF THE DRAGON'S DRUM

the Strait is found in Chaplain's Fletcher's notes and drawings. In these can be found sketches of the seeming endless supply of sea birds that ensured the crew remained well nourished during the month they made their way westward. Magellan had dubbed the amusing birds geese, but Welshmen in the crew had a more fitting name. They would be known from that day forward as "pen gwinns" or white shirts.

On August 29 the *Golden Hind* and the other ships met the full furry of the turbulent winds Magellan wrote about years before. "The mountains," writes Fletcher, "being very high and some reaching into the frozen region did every one send out their several winds; sometimes behind us to send us in our way, sometimes on the starboard side to drive us to the larboard and so the contrary; sometimes right against us to drive us further back in an hour than we could recover again in many. But of all others this was the worse: that sometime two or three of these winds would come together and meet as it was, in one body, whose forces being become one, did so violently fall into the sea, whirling, or as the Spaniard sayeth, a Tornado, that they would pierce into the very bowels of the sea and make it swell upwards on every side. The hollowness they made in the water and the winds breaking out again, did take the swelling banks so raised into the air, and being dispersed abroad it ran down again a mighty rain. Besides this, the sea is so deep in all this passage that upon life and death there is no coming to anchor." The water was fierce, but Fletcher returned his thoughts to the mountains: "Neither may I omit the grisly sight of the cold and frozen mountains, reaching their heads, yea the greatest part of their bodies into the cold and frozen region, where the power of the reflection of the Sun never toucheth to dissolve the ice and snow, so that the ice and snow hang about the spire of the

Francis Drake   Echoes of the Dragon's Drum

mountain circularwise as it were regions, by degrees one above another and one exceeding another in breadth, in a wonderful order."[59]

Though Drake made record time in his journey through the Strait, for him, like all captains before him, there was a heavy toll. As the *Golden Hind* entered the Pacific in September, it sailed alone. One ship had sunk, and one manned by Captain Winter had returned for England, something for which Drake never forgave him. Nearly half of his men had perished, but he pressed on for the prize that lay before him. Northward lay Peru and the Spanish treasure ships, fat with gold and manned by overconfident sailors accustomed to having the Pacific all to themselves.

Finishing the Course (1578-80)

The general minding to depart
Commands his men in haste aboard,
Then lifting up both hands and heart
Most thankfully they praise the Lord,
For giving them such victory
Without bloodshed or jeopardy.

—Thomas Greepe

With his remaining ship and diminished crew, Drake turned his attention to the Spanish sea towns and coastal villages of the West Coast of South America. As he had done in the Atlantic, he captured Spanish ships and pressed those he could into service. He planned to hit hard and fast then move on before word could reach his next target. Everything went according to plan until Drake stopped at Mocha Island. The locals there knew European visitors all too well and apparently assumed Drake and his men to be no different than the Spanish. According to journals from the voyage:

"When Francis Drake had passed the Straits of Magellan, the first land he fell with was an island named Mocha, where he came to an anchor, and hoisting out his boat, he, with ten of his company, went on shore, thinking there to have taken in freshwater. Two of the company, going

FRANCIS DRAKE   ECHOES OF THE DRAGON'S DRUM

far into the island were intercepted and cut off by the Indians that inhabit the island, who, as some as then saw our men come to anchor, thought they would come on land (as they did indeed), and laid an ambush of about 100 Indians; and where our boat was fast on ground and all the men gone on land, the ambush broke out and set upon them, and before they could recover their boat and get her on float, they hurt all our men very sore with their arrows....

"More died of their wounds, the rest escaped their wounds and were cured. They stayed here but one day, but set sail toward the coast of Chile, where arriving they met with an Indian in a canoe near the shore, who thinking them to have been Spaniards, told them that behind there, at a place called St. Yago, there was a Spanish ship, for which good news they gave him diverse trifles. The Indians being joyful thereof went on shore and brought them ... sheep and a small quantity of fish, and so they returned back again to St. Yago to seek the Spanish ship (for they overshot the place before they were ware); and when they came thither, they found the same ship."[60]

By now, Drake had fewer than 80 men left, and many of them suffered from scurvy. As the *Golden Hind* headed north, Drake's men skirmished with locals, two more sailors died, and twice arrows wounded the Captain himself. It had been a long arduous journey filled with more disappointment than success, but on December 5, the tide turned. Drake struck the Spanish port town of Valparaiso and captured the *La Capitana*, a merchant ship laden with enough gold, silver, and jewels to more than pay for the entire expedition. Drake's men celebrated and lauded their

FRANCIS DRAKE — ECHOES OF THE DRAGON'S DRUM

captain's leadership, and the victory whetted their leader's appetite for more plunder and revenge.

With the capture of the *La Capatina*, Drake had a fleet again. He had also captured the accurate charts he needed to make a successful assault on the rest of South America and to move north to find the fabled Northwest Passage above North America. Before moving on, he searched out a protected bay and oversaw the work of making proper repairs to his flagship. By mid-January, the three vessels were ready to move up the coast of Peru where in only a few days he netted the equivalent of $10 million in gold before catching wind of an even bigger prize. Rumors from captured Spaniards led Drake to head out in pursuit of the *Nuestra Senora de la Concepcion*, which was bound for Manila laden with treasure. After a bit of subterfuge and much daring, the *Golden Hind* caught up to its lumbering target and netted a greater treasure than that of the *La Capitana*. Drake had 80 more pounds of gold and 26 tons of silver to share among his investors, gentlemen, his own coffers, and of course, the Queen.

By the spring of 1579, news of El Draco spread like wildfire throughout South and Central America and word filtered back to Europe about his doings. Eight months after deserting Drake in the Strait of Magellan, John Winter arrived in Devon on June 2, 1579 and quickly dispatched a confidential report defending his decision to turn back. On June 10 the Spanish ambassador in London wrote a report to King Philip containing accurate accounts of Drake's voyage up to the point where Winter had become separated from him, including the trial and execution of Thomas Doughty. During the first week in August of that same year

FRANCIS DRAKE ECHOES OF THE DRAGON'S DRUM

the Spanish treasure fleet arrived in Seville with report of Drake's raids. From Nicaragua one official lamented, "It is a thing that terrifies one, this voyage and the boldness of this low man." From Mexico, Don Martin Enriquez advised Philip take immediate steps to prevent further intrusions. "Now Your Majesty will see how important it is that this sea should have security, and will give orders to safeguard that strait which affords a troublesome entrance to this country, Peru and China." Don Antonio de Padilla, president of Philip's Council of the Indies, advised, "This matter much deserves great deliberation not only on account of the present case … but also in view of the future."[61] On August 11, after reading the opinion of the Audiencia of Panama that Drake planned to escape by way of the Moluccas and the Portuguese route around the Cape of Good Hope, Philip asked King Henry of Portugal, to issue an order to intercept him in the East Indies.

Meanwhile, the *Golden Hind* continued northward coming at last to Mexico. During this time, he captured many prisoners and released most. Experienced navigators he pressed into his service and, more often than not, they accepted their new position well. That is not to say that Drake never threatened nor tortured a few; he did. Always dashing, he was just as likely to release captured mariners with lavish gifts to compensate for their trouble. Even so, he proselytized with great zeal, using his beloved *Foxe's Book of Martyrs* to illustrate the barbaric treatment of Protestants by Rome. When ashore, his men looted churches, smashed icons, and taunted priests mercilessly. But in truth, released sailors had to more to fear from the Inquisition than Francis Drake. Many such men came under suspicion of being infected with what the Roman Catholic Church considered a false gospel championed by a heretic

FRANCIS DRAKE   ECHOES OF THE DRAGON'S DRUM

queen. Unfortunately for them, the Inquisition tended to torture first and forgive later (if forgiveness came at all).

Drake's exploits in capturing treasure-laden ships over so much territory with just a single vessel created a tempest of fear and dread that swept before him. The moment El Draque appeared, Spanish governors mobilized their territories and ordered warships to pursue the elusive "devil ship." Former prisoners spread the tale to all who would listen that this pirate was the English dragon who ravaged ships and villages on the Spanish Main. They claimed he had many great vessels that rode low in the water beneath numerous cannon and that his decks swarmed with hundreds if not thousands of Protestant devils. Though Spanish authorities urged aggressive pursuit, the rumors gained strength until they were fact in the mind of captains who weighed a chance at glory against survival. As a result, the fervor for finding Drake waned until few dared look.

The capture of the Cacafuego.

Unhindered by enemies, Drake set his sights on the greatest prize of all—the Spanish treasure ship, *Cacafuego*. Taking the ship proved easier than expected, and Drake's men boarded with little loss of life. With its cargo of gold, silver, and jewels, the *Cacafuego* gave England the most valuable prize ever captured by any of Elizabeth's Sea Dogs. If Drake's sailors

FRANCIS DRAKE　　ECHOES OF THE DRAGON'S DRUM

were not loyal before, this day ensured they would be as he gave each a portion of the gold and silver plates they captured.

Though Drake could be as harsh as any sea captain when the situation demanded it, he also showed unusual grace toward many of the Spanish and Portuguese he captured during his voyages. William Wood offers a brief insight into Drake's treatment of Don Anton, the captain of the *Cacafuego*:

> *"The prisoners were no less gratified than surprised by Drake's kind treatment. He entertained Don Anton at a banquet, took him all over the Golden Hind, and entrusted him with a message to Don Martin, the traitor of San Juan de Ulúa. Namely, if Don Martin hanged any more Englishmen, as he had Oxenham, he should soon be given a present of two thousand Spanish heads. Then Drake gave every Spanish officer and man a personal gift proportioned to his rank, put all his accumulated prisoners aboard the emptied treasure ship, wished them a prosperous voyage and better luck next time, furnished the brave Don Anton with a letter of protection in case he should fall in with an English vessel, and, after many expressions of goodwill on both sides, Drake sailed north, the voyage 'made'; while the poor 'spit-silver' treasure ship turned sadly east and steered for Panama."*[62]

A few days later, captured prisoners, fresh from Spain, offered a prize nearly as valuable as gold when they provided the first news Drake and his men had heard of their homeland since embarking from Plymouth more than year earlier. As Dudley writes: "The crew feasted and celebrated when they learned that all was right with their world.

FRANCIS DRAKE — ECHOES OF THE DRAGON'S DRUM

The Protestant Netherlands still resisted their Spanish overlord, French Catholics still murdered French Huguenots, and Elizabeth had neither reconciled nor (God forbid it!) married a Catholic prince. Though singing and dancing at the news of increasing European religious fratricide may seem strange, every man knew that a severe outbreak of peace would have branded the expedition as pirates, to be despised, hunted, and happily executed by all European nations."[63]

Once the rejoicing subsided, Drake knew he must make a difficult decision. With his hold filled with plunder, returning home by the way he had come was out of the question. Every town, garrison, and ship was alert to his presence and surely prepared should he come their way again. Added to that, no captain, not even Drake, had the audacity to attempt another run at the Strait of Magellan so quickly. A second option was to follow the path of Magellan, sail toward the Philippines, and then circumnavigate the world. But the allure of the possibility of a northwest passage was too great for any Englishman, so Drake steered the *Golden Hind* toward Canada in search of the mythical Strait of Anian, a way from the Pacific to the Atlantic. In late April 1579, somewhere along the coast of modern Canada, storms and contrary winds forced Drake to abandon his search. Instead, he sought a quiet bay in which to refurbish his vessels, replenish his supplies, and rest his men before attempting the feat that a half-century earlier had cost Magellan four of five ships, all but a handful of his crew, and his ultimately his own life.

Though the exact location remains the topic of debate, Drake found a quiet bay in early June somewhere near present-day San Francisco.

FRANCIS DRAKE   ECHOES OF THE DRAGON'S DRUM

Mindful of lessons learned from his earlier encounters with natives on Mocha Island, Drake took care to avoid trouble with the locals of this unexplored land. Chaplain Fletcher wrote in his diary on June 21 of the crew's encounter with the local natives that lived in the area:

"On this day the ship was brought near shore and anchored. Goods were landed, and some sort of stone fortification was erected for defense. The Indians made their appearance in increasing numbers until there was a 'great number of both men and women.' It is clearly apparent that the natives were not simply curious, but acted, as Fletcher points out, 'as men ravished in their minds' and 'their errand being rather with submission and fear to worship us as Gods, than to have any war with us as mortal men.' It would seem that the natives demonstrated clearly their fear and wonderment at the English, and it is certain that they behaved as no other natives had done in the experience of the chronicler. The English gave their visitors shirts and line cloth, in return for which (as Fletcher thought) the Indians presented to Drake and some of the English such things as feathers, net caps, quivers for arrows, and animal skins which the women wore. Then, having visited for a time, the natives left for their homes about three-quarters of a mile away. As soon as they were home, the Indians began to lament, 'extending their voices, in a most miserable and doleful manner of shrieking.'

"Inserted between the passages dealing with the departure of the Indians to their homes and their lamenting is a description of their houses and dress. The houses are described as 'digged round within the earth, and have the uppermost brims of the circle, clefts of wood set

Francis Drake   Echoes of the Dragon's Drum

New Albion. English galleon "Golden Hinde" Oil on canvas. 60 x 90 cm by Simon Kozhin 2007. Courtesy of Simon KozhinКожин, Семён Леонидович, Wikimedia Commons.

up, and joined close together at the top, like our spires on the steep of a church: which being covered with earth, suffer no water enter, and are very warm, the door in the most part of them, performs the office of a chimney, to let out the smoke: its made in bigness and fashion, like to an ordinary scuttle in a ship, and standing slopewise: their beds are the hard ground, only with rushed strewn upon it, and lying round about the house, have their fire in the midst.'

"The men are for the most part naked, and the women wore a shredded

FRANCIS DRAKE — ECHOES OF THE DRAGON'S DRUM

bullrush . . . skirt which hung around the hips. Women also wore a shoulder cape of deerskin with the hair upon it."[64]

Drake's cousin later related their interactions with the Native Americans:

"There he [Francis Drake] landed and built huts and remained a month and a half, caulking his vessel. The victuals they found were mussels and sea-lions. During that time many Indians came there and when they saw the Englishmen they wept and scratched their faces with their nails until they drew blood, as though this were an act of homage or adoration. By signs Captain Francis told them not to do that, for the Englishmen were not God. These people were peaceful and did no harm to the English, but gave them no food. They are of the color of the Indians here (Peru) and are comely. They carry bows and arrows and go naked. The climate is temperate, more cold than not. To all appearance it is a very good country. Here he caulked his large ship and left the ship he had taken in Nicaragua. He departed, leaving the Indians, to all appearance, sad."[65]

With his ships repaired and stores replenished, it was time to complete the historic journey. Before leaving, Drake claimed the land and named it Nova Albion or New Britain. Thus, the original New England lay on the west coast of North America rather than the east. Sketchy records indicate that Drake left a small party behind to establish a colony. However, due to the secrecy of his mission it appears that Drake altered his records in case the Spanish happened on them. What became of the colony is lost to history. As for Drake and the *Golden Hind*, thousands

FRANCIS DRAKE — ECHOES OF THE DRAGON'S DRUM

of miles of the Pacific lay between them and England.

In November 1579, seven months after any European had heard word of Francis Drake, a Portuguese galleon encountered the *Golden Hind* south of the Philippines. At first Drake thought to engage the ship, but instead made his way south of the Philippines to the Moluccas, often known as the famous Spice Islands. The Portuguese's treatment of the locals, they were told, outdid the Spanish. A year earlier, Lopez de Mosquito murdered the Sultan, chopped up the body, and threw it into the sea. The Sultan's son, Baber, had driven out the Portuguese from the island of Ternate and was making preparations to do the same on the the island of Tidore, when Drake arrived. The new Sultan offered Queen Elizabeth, via Drake, a complete monopoly of the trade in spices if only he would use the *Golden Hind* as the flagship in doing battle against the Portuguese. As tempting as the opportunity might be, Drake knew that his crew, now down to 56 men, faced too much ahead of them to remain and engage the Portuguese. So he traded for all the spices he could stow away and established an understanding with the Sultan that formed the foundation of English diplomacy in Eastern seas for another century to come. Elizabeth was later so pleased with this result that she gave Drake a cup engraved with a picture of his reception by the Sultan Baber of Ternate.

Another eight months passed before definite word of the Drake expedition reached first Spain and then England. It was late summer, and Drake had made it as far north as the coast of France. On July 29, 1580, Pedro de Rada wrote:

FRANCIS DRAKE   ECHOES OF THE DRAGON'S DRUM

"Very Illustrious Lord,

"Having, as was my duty, exerted vigilance in order to ascertain what success has been obtained by the Captain Francis, English Corsair, who entered the South Sea, I obtained the following from two inhabitants of this town, both masters of vessels and persons of credit who had arrived from Nantes in France.

"There, two Frenchmen, whom I also knew to be reliable, who habitually come to this port and are now expected daily, told them and certified that the said Captain Francis, Englishman, with the same ship which had entered the South Sea, had come to Belle Isle in France, about 30 miles from la Rochelle in the mouth of the entrance to Nantes, and had brought a great quantity of treasure of gold and silver, a part of which he had unloaded secretly on the said Island and transported to the mainland of France.

"After remaining therefore about six days, he had gone to la Rochelle and Antioche which is in the same straits of la Rochelle, and there [the two Frenchmen] had learnt, from his own lips, how he had entered the self-same strait of Magellan and passed through it into the South Sea, and that he had not dared to go to England on account of having beheaded a noble gentleman whom he had carried in his company, and for other reasons.

"Although I am now awaiting the arrival of these French shipmasters, in order to obtain from them the most authentic account possible, it seemed to me advisable to inform Your Grace of what has been related..."[66]

On August 19, de Rada wrote again:

"The French shipmasters whom I was expecting in order to obtain all the information I could, have arrived here. They state that an English ship of approximately 200 tons, with much artillery and a great quantity of silver and gold had arrived at Belle Isle de Saint Jean.

"He had stayed at La Rochelle on his way, in search of some place where he could repair and clean his ship because it came covered with a superabundance of long seaweed, such as grows of its own accord on the vessels that navigate in the Indian Seas.

"Therefore, without sailing much, he was searching for a suitable careening place in the islands of Houat which I myself have visited. They are uninhabited and situated between Morbihan in France and the entrance to the coast of Nantes.

"When the Captains of the galleys of France heard of him, two of the galleys which patrol the coast attacked and fought him, not knowing who he was or what wealth he carried—but merely on the supposition that he was a Corsair.

"He defended himself, however, and sailed for a second time towards la Rochelle.

"It is believed that he was keeping about that coast, entertaining himself, until he received word from England, whither he had sent a message in order to ensure a safe return to that realm."[67]

FRANCIS DRAKE   ECHOES OF THE DRAGON'S DRUM

There was no doubt now; Francis Drake and the few men that remained with him soon would be home. However, de Rada's letters prove that Drake was following a familiar script of misdirection and intrigue. It is highly doubtful, barring some catastrophe, that the voyage from the Philippines took anywhere near the amount of time indicated. Drake undoubtedly completed a much quicker passage home than any account of the voyage admits. Certainly, he could not have spent six months meandering through the East Indies or left from Java any later than mid-February. There is no doubt that Drake made it to the coast of France much earlier than supposed and waited there to unload and hide some of his plunder and receive word that it was safe to proceed across the Channel.

For most in England, news of Drake's imminent return invoked great celebration. It had been months since any sure word of the fate of the *Golden Hind* surfaced, and rumors of wildly varying possibilities abounded. With the hanging of John Oxenham at Lima came rumor the Francis Drake had been hanged as well. Captain Winter, unwilling to admit the real reason he turned the *Elizabeth* away from the Strait of Magellan and fled home, let it be assumed that the *Golden Hind* had not survived the passage. His return in 1578 with nothing but bad news had been followed with no news at all of Drake from Peru or Mexico the next year. By 1580, Drake's friends, supporters, and investors began to fear the worse. During those same months the Spanish rejoiced, hoping the hated Dragon lay at the bottom of the sea or better yet in some Guinea cannibal's belly.

Finally, after almost three years traversing the world, Francis Drake and

FRANCIS DRAKE   ECHOES OF THE DRAGON'S DRUM

the crew of the *Golden Hind* entered the familiar waters of Plymouth Sound. On September 26, 1580, fishermen in a barque much like the one in which a ten year old Drake had first learned to love the sea spotted a weather-beaten vessel riding dangerously low in the water. As they hailed the ship, they saw fifty-seven equally weather-beaten men gazing with longing eyes at the shores of Plymouth. Francis Drake yelled to the fishermen, "Is the Queen alive?"

The men in the barque answered in the affirmative, and though Drake and his men rejoiced, they did not rush home. Both the politics of the day and the legendary fickleness of Elizabeth made any privateer wary, and Drake was returning from no ordinary mission. As the *Golden Hind* remained anchored in the bay, the people of Plymouth celebrated the return of their favorite son. But even as many rejoiced, many more mourned. 163 had left with high hopes of trade and profit, and over a hundred did not return. Drake's wife, Mary, ferried out to see the husband she shared with the sea. Only months after his first series of voyages to the Spanish Main, Drake had spent a scant few months enjoying married life before heading off on his secret mission with, as Dudley so aptly puts it, "his lifelong mistress the sea."[68]

Even once the *Golden Hind* docked, Drake moved forward with caution. To a modern observer, it would seem a parade at the dock was in order. Surely there would be ticker tape (had such a thing existed) and musicians and glowing political speeches to be followed by a gala ball, and a command appearance before the Queen. But Drake's first question on spotting countrymen came with good reason. Had Elizabeth died before his return or if had she made some new pact with Philip of

FRANCIS DRAKE — ECHOES OF THE DRAGON'S DRUM

Spain, the brash captain and his crew might well be facing a hangman's noose or the axe. The first issue was settled; the Queen lived! It took a few weeks to ascertain the answer to his second question.

After testing of the political waters, Drake answered a summons from the Queen to come to London. He took with him a select portion of his plunders in the Pacific, the total value of which amounted to the equivalent of upwards of $100 million. Drake and all of his men were rich from their share, and what he carried to Elizabeth amounted to over half of her entire budget for the coming year. He placed select treasures at her feet and for six hours captivated his Queen with details of his voyage. By the time Francis Drake left London the next day, he stood as Elizabeth's favorite Sea Dog with his place established among the greats of British history.

FRANCIS DRAKE — ECHOES OF THE DRAGON'S DRUM

A Commoner among Gentleman

Sir Drake, whom well the world's ends know,
Which thou didst compass round,
And whom both poles of heaven once saw
Which North and South do bound.
The stars above will make thee known,
If men here silent were,
The sun himself cannot forget
His fellow traveller.

—Anonymous

Drake not only returned from his famous voyage with treasure, but also with word that he had claimed New Avalon (the American Northwest) for the Queen and England. The question of his right to claim territory for England posed as much a problem for Elizabeth as all of Drake's plundering and retribution combined. His triumphal return from circumnavigating the globe brought a hero's welcome from the people of England, but a tempest of protest from the Spanish ambassador. After all, the pope had declared anything "beyond the line" as the sole property of Spain, and therefore England had no legal right to New Avalon or any other lands in the New World. Drake was probably thankful he did not have to take part in the legal and political wrangling his exploits created.

FRANCIS DRAKE — ECHOES OF THE DRAGON'S DRUM

Queen Elizabeth countered Spain's protests on two fronts: the law of prior right and that of possession. Some years earlier, she had employed John Dee, a trusted advisor, to provide her with some legal argument to defend England's right to explore and colonize North America. Dee was a self-taught scholar and the Queen's personal astrologer. After extensive research in Justinian Law and Arthurian myth, he concluded England had rights to North America that preceded Spain's by a thousand years. The Arthurian argument was sketchy at best, but the one he based on Justinian Law was not. Dee appealed to ancient legal precedent. Spain may have asserted her sovereignty over the northern parts of America, but she had done nothing to occupy the land; and physical occupation, under Roman law, was an essential part of establishing legal title.

In spite of intense Spanish protests and internal political pressure, Elisabeth knew she could not belittle or ignore the contribution her Sea Dog had made to England. His daring now filled her war coffers, ensuring she could defend herself against Spain's inevitable assault on the island nation. A storm of protests from Philip and British merchants who stood to lose a fortune in a trade with Spain, assaulted London daily, but in the end Francis Drake's standing as a national hero remained firm.

After her initial meeting with Drake upon his return, Elizabeth made an edict that only she and her most trusted ministers were to review the records of his journeys. Any member of the crew that shared specifics of their adventure risked execution. The Queen insisted that nothing Drake learned on his voyage about geography or Spanish capabilities should fall into the hands of the Spain and its many spies.

FRANCIS DRAKE   ECHOES OF THE DRAGON'S DRUM

Though he was now a wealthy man and in the good graces of the Queen, it still took a surprisingly long time for the public to accept Drake's account of his adventures. Drake's voyage through the Strait of Magellan and storm-inspired detour in the South Sea between South America and Antarctica provided a possible way to avoid the dangerous and now heavily defended Strait altogether. However, neither this nor his discoveries in the Pacific northwest gained much publicity, and when Thomas Cavendish, the next circumnavigator, failed to confirm the string of islands south of the Magellan Strait, geographers began to doubt the accuracy of Drake's accounts. It would not be until two decades after Drake's death that the Dutchmen Le Marie and Schouten confirmed Drake's findings.

However, even among Drake's detractors, the Spanish included, none doubted the significance of the feat he had accomplished or the place he would forever hold in the English imagination. Sugden explains:

> *"Everyone knew that Drake had made a difference. As a feat of navigation alone his voyage was unsurpassed by any of the great age of discovery. Thomas Blundeville estimated in 1594 that the expedition had traversed 36,000 miles, or the equivalent of more than one and two-thirds circuits of the Equator. It dwarfed any of the voyages of Columbus and Vasco da Gama, and was substantially longer than either the first or third circumnavigations by Magellan or Cavendish respectively; and it had not been done by Iberian seamen, the acknowledged masters of oceanic exploration, but by Englishmen who had never before broken the bounds of the Atlantic. Although Drake had used rudders, maps and local pilots, and although he left the routine handling of the ship*

FRANCIS DRAKE ECHOES OF THE DRAGON'S DRUM

to his subordinates (Simon Wood and William Hawkins, two of his men, said that the commander often retired to his cabin at eight in the evening and that he would stir thereafter for neither wind nor rain), the bulk of the credit for the navigation belonged to Sir Francis. No pilots had served him on those mighty hauls across the Pacific and Indian oceans; none of his charts or rudders gave more than an inkling of the intricacies of the Strait of Magellan or the Celebes Sea; and for many regions he had had no guidance whatsoever. He had found his maps as much misleading as helpful. When pilots were available, Drake preferred his own judgement. As he told one of them, the pilot need do no more than point out the landmarks, for he would see to the rest. The best navigators of the day, men like the Spaniard Pedro Sarmiento de Gamboa, the Portuguese Nuño da Silva, and the Englishman John Davis, attested to Drake's mastery of their trade, and, of course, none was more aware of this than Drake himself. He boasted 'of being such a good sailor, so learned, that . . . there was no one in the world who understood better the art of sailing.' In public estimation the voyage proved him right. Edmund Howes, in an edition of John Stow's Chronicles, saw Drake as 'more skilful in all points of navigation than any that ever was before his time, in his time, or since his death. He was also of perfect memory, great observation, eloquent by nature, skilful in artillery, expert and apt to let blood and give physic unto his people according to the climates.'"[69]

Drake's voyage suggested that England had come of age as a maritime power and fostered inspiration for further Elizabethan endeavor. However, even here we must be careful not to exaggerate its initial

FRANCIS DRAKE   ECHOES OF THE DRAGON'S DRUM

impact. Philip responded, not for the first or the last time, to Drake's opportunism, and in 1581 sent an expedition of some 3,500 men in 23 ships under Diego Flores de Valdes with orders to occupy the River Plate region and the Strait of Magellan and to reinforce Chile. The venture was disastrous, for few of the men saw their native land again, and it took only a few years to reduce the colony at the strait to a pathetic, starving remnant. Nevertheless, it deterred the English from developing a trade with Brazil. Better service was done Spain by a new royal South Seas fleet established in the 1580s. In 1587, Thomas Cavendish tried to emulate Sir Francis. But without Drake's flair and Providence's favor, he lost thirty men skirmishing with the Spaniards and gained far fewer rewards. By the time the next intruder, Richard Hawkins, arrived, the Spanish were ready and forced him to surrender on the coast of Ecuador in 1594.

Drake's success resulted in Spain's improved defenses; England could not carry out her ambition of repeating Drake's great voyage. "There was plenty of spirit, true enough. Mendoza complained that 'at present there is hardly an Englishman who is not talking of undertaking the voyage, so encouraged are they by Drake's return.' But success was not forthcoming. Humphrey Gilbert and two of his ships' companies perished in the icy seas of the north Atlantic attempting to colonize Newfoundland. Davis's search for the North-west Passage in the 1580s likewise failed, and Raleigh, who took up Gilbert's patent and tried to establish settlements in Virginia, was ultimately no more successful. Captain Fenton's efforts to capitalize on Drake's agreement with Ternate ended in a shambles, and he returned to England empty-handed and his expedition in pieces. If Drake had proved that Englishmen could

FRANCIS DRAKE   ECHOES OF THE DRAGON'S DRUM

sail anywhere, his countrymen waited long to demonstrate that the great voyage had not been something of a freak, an unusual stroke of genius aided by good fortune. Until Drake himself put to sea again and Cavendish made the third circumnavigation there was little enough for English expansionists to exult about. The disappointing years that immediately followed Drake's voyage around the world, the inability of the English to transform their triumph into a regular South American or East Indian trade, left the promise of the voyage unfulfilled but its status as a symbol of individual endeavour the greater. Against its context, it shone brighter still."[70]

Francis Drake's share of gold and silver plate from his expedition in the Pacific made him one of the wealthiest men in England, and his bold exploits made him the most famous. With his substantial share of the plunder, Drake obtained a large manor in Devon, which he named Buckland Abbey. When not at sea, he spent the remaining years of life there along with frequent trips to London where he basked in his new found fame and standing with the Queen.

Drake was not above moments of grandiosity, which jealous rivals called arrogance. However, confidence is often confused with arrogance, and in Elizabethan England, confidence from a former commoner was insufferable. Thus, some accused Drake of extravagance when he presented the Queen with a special jewel from his treasure. It was a pendant made from gold captured off the coast of Mexico and set with a diamond mined in Africa and a small ship carved from ebony. Even more vexing to the snobbish in Elizabeth's court was the gift she gave Drake in return. Known as "Drake's Jewel," her gift bore a miniature

FRANCIS DRAKE — ECHOES OF THE DRAGON'S DRUM

portrait of herself set in a jeweled frame. On the back of the jewel was a cameo of twin busts of a royal woman and an African man. Elizabeth's gift remained Drake's most prized possession as long as he lived and in many ways symbolized how far he had risen.

Regardless of the opposition he encountered from the wealthy elite in England, Francis Drake never returned to the status of insignificant commoner again. When Queen Elizabeth knighted him, he entered territory no boy of the Devon backwaters dared dream. By the age of 40, he had conquered the world and risen to the status of knight and gentleman. This former river rat, by the grace of God and the favor of the Queen, had accomplished everything he had ever imagined. Bloody Mary's reign of terror and the Catholic counter-reformation, his family's flight from the land of its heritage, and the full vengeance of Philip's mighty galleons could not snatch away his personal manifest destiny.

M. DE L'ACADEMIE ROYALE des SCIENCES
et quelques autres et sur les memoires les plus recens
PAR M. DE L'ISLE

Part V

Mortality Becomes Immortal

Mrs de l'Academie Royale des Sciences
et quelques autres et sur les memoires les plus recens
Par M. de l'Isle

FRANCIS DRAKE — ECHOES OF THE DRAGON'S DRUM

It is good news, and now I will get well.

—Philip II on word of the death of Francis Drake

Two of the most notable character traits of Francis Drake were his devotion to God and country and his admiration for faithful work. He rose from nothing through hard work, and he respected those who put themselves to the same thing. As a contemporary put it, "the good captain measured others by what they could accomplish on a day-to-day basis; and the ability to write a sonnet or to parse a Greek verb mattered not at all to a sailor and a warrior. Rather the man who could quickly reef a sail, splice a stay, or caulk a plank by day, then fearlessly wield a pile or bow . . . excited the admiration of Drake."[71] Equally important to Drake was unfailing loyalty. He wasn't above seeking to buy it with gold and silver and on a few occasions with the sword. But a captain of the seas must know how to command respect, and Francis Drake had learned that lesson well.

Back at home that respect could not be won so easily. Drake's proven abilities mattered little, while his attempts to buy his way into the hearts of his detractors floundered. Drake's elevation to the ranks of near nobility brought him into contact with a new kind of Englishman. Themselves born to wealth and luxury, many viewed Drake as a vulgar upstart, a creature of the dirty masses who had stolen his way into their society. Drake learned the lessons of English class as a boy, and now he must learn them from a different point of view. To earn a title did not mean acceptance by those who were born with one. As Dudley so eloquently

FRANCIS DRAKE ⚓ ECHOES OF THE DRAGON'S DRUM

put it, the reverse of every medal of honor should be "inscribed with the words jealousy and scorn."[72] Regardless of the Queen's favor and his own wealth, Drake continued to face opposition from the nobleman as well as career officers of the Royal Navy. But it would be men like Drake, men they considered to be rogues and dirty commoners, that England would soon call on to preserve its very existence from a furious Spanish king.

Modern biographers often psychoanalyze Drake, seeking to determine what motivated and molded him. But in the end, the totality of his actions is a more trustworthy measure. There is no doubt that Francis Drake was driven by something beyond average ambition, but then again he was no average man. At this stage of his life, he could have lived out his life as a national hero. However, such was not the stuff of which he was made. The final chapter of Drake's life would prove to be a time of his greatest successes and failures. And it is in both of those that his legend grew to proportions that the passage of centuries has done little to dull.

FRANCIS DRAKE — Echoes of the Dragon's Drum

Singeing King Philip's Beard (1581-1587)

*And in your fighting evermore,
think you are Englishmen,
Then every one of you
I hope will slay of Spaniards ten,
Or any else whatever they be,
that shall disturb your peace
And seek by any kind of mean your quiet to decease.*

—Henry Roberts

Just as Drake settled into private life at Buckland Abbey, Mary, his wife of twelve years, died. Records reveal that this tragedy might have been the results of complications during pregnancy. Well over half of their marriage had seen them separated by the ocean and Drake's insatiable desire to see Spain stopped abroad and at home. For the next three years he showed no interest in remarrying and instead set his sights on politics. In September of 1581, he was installed as mayor of Plymouth and then won a seat in Parliament, representing Camelford. Several years later, he won reelection, this time representing Bossiney.

In spite of his accomplishments both at sea and at home, Francis Drake remained an outsider. With all of its advancements, Elizabethan England was still run by gentlemen and nobility of which he was neither.

FRANCIS DRAKE   ECHOES OF THE DRAGON'S DRUM

To them, his exploits and proven abilities mattered little. So Drake put his sizable share of Spanish plunder to work giving lavish gifts anywhere he thought it might curry favor and acceptance. With some the tactic was successful; with others it was not.

Firmly established in his new role of public official, Drake finally considered marriage. Mary's standing in society had been so slight that records hardly remain as to her existence before marrying Francis, but Elizabeth Sydenham, Drake's second wife, was the only living child of the High Sheriff of Somerset, Sir George Sydenham. They would remain married until Drake's death, but like Mary before her, Elizabeth never bore Drake a child to whom he could leave his legacy.

Francis Drake's second wife, Elizabeth Sydenham.

Mary and Elizabeth were quite different: one a commoner, the other from status. However, the on-again, off-again problems between Spain and England ensured that Elizabeth and Mary had one thing in common. Both spent their married lives as relative strangers to the man who pursued his first love, the sea. Five years had passed since Drake returned from the New World, and now Elizabeth approached Drake with a new mission. Unlike the clandestine voyage on the *Golden Hind*,

FRANCIS DRAKE — ECHOES OF THE DRAGON'S DRUM

Elizabeth had something much bigger in mind. She needed the one man whose experience suited the gambit she was considering. She wanted Francis Drake to lead an all-out raiding mission on the Spanish Main.

Many historians portray the raids as pre-emptive—an effort to launch a crippling blow against Spain before it could begin hostilities against England. In truth, Elizabeth's advisors envisioned the expedition as one last hope for peace. Drake was to provide the kind of quick and decisive action at the source of Spain's wealth necessary to force King Philip's to give up his expansionist intentions.

As Konstam writes: "The raid . . . came within a hair's breadth of being called off, as Elizabeth began to have second thoughts. Ever the opportunist, Drake solved the Queen's problem by sailing anyway, before Elizabeth could change her mind. What followed became the stuff of legend, a dramatic stab against the very heart of Spain's overseas empire. Drake was in his element, and this proved to be his finest hour. His earlier forays into the Caribbean had been mere pinpricks. This was a rapier thrust. His foray into the Pacific earned him a fortune in plunder, but this raid was on a different scale entirely. Rather than commanding a single ship, Drake led a whole invasion force, ready and willing to cause as much destruction as they could, and his men were eager for treasure. After all, like all raids of this kind this was as much a business speculation as a military adventure, and with the Queen as his main financial backer, Drake not only had to strike hard against the Spanish, but he also had to turn a profit. This then, would be the wily Sea Dog's greatest test."[73]

FRANCIS DRAKE — ECHOES OF THE DRAGON'S DRUM

The stakes were high for Elizabeth. Failure meant the loss of her kingdom and quite possibly her life. But she also had much to gain. With war to wage, King Philip II needed money—enormous sums of it. His biggest source of such revenue lay in the gold mines of Colombia, the emerald fields of Venezuela, and the silver mines of Peru and Mexico. Every year a portion of these great riches was taken to the ports of the Spanish Main, and from there they were shipped to Spain in its famous treasure fleets. Queen Elizabeth hoped that by seizing the ports she could capture the treasure. If Drake succeeded, the result would be two-fold: Philip would be denied the money he needed to strike at England, and Elizabeth could fill her war coffers, ensuring the proper defense her country so desperately needed. The plan was daring and diplomatically risky, but Elizabeth saw no other way to stop Spain. Drake had been to the New World on three different campaigns: once with his cousin John Hawkins, again when he first made Spain suffer the loss of its fabled treasure, and finally during his year and a half of plundering Spanish treasure ships in the Pacific. None of them matched in importance what Elizabeth called on him to do in 1585.

To appreciate the impact of the assault, consider how the Sea Dogs operated before this time. By formally acknowledging the man Queen Elizabeth called "my pirate," she was sending an unmistakable signal to the Spanish that English attitudes toward them had entered a new and more resolute phase. For years Drake and his compatriots had tread a diplomatic tightrope while Spain and England engaged in a cold war. With the Queen's public announcement that Francis Drake was to lead a very public and well-financed mission to the Spanish Main, there could be no doubt that diplomatic niceties had reached their limit. Drake's

FRANCIS DRAKE   ECHOES OF THE DRAGON'S DRUM

private war with the Spanish escalated into an international struggle.

Like all naval military enterprises of the day, the expedition was a joint-stock enterprise. That meant that individuals put up a stake in the venture, either in money, ships, men, or resources. Every stakeholder expected a return in the form of a share of the plunder. Some estimate that the stakeholders in Drake's voyage around the world realized a profit of 41 to 1. This expedition was therefore not only a great privateering raid—it was a commercial enterprise, with specific goals. If Drake succeeded, the gain his investors realized from plunder would also deprive the Spanish of the resources they needed to wage war and increase England's own ability to defend herself and her allies.

As admiral, Drake commanded an impressive force of 29 ships. His vice-admiral, Martin Frobisher, was an experienced and notoriously hard-nosed seaman who had already made his mark as a privateer and Arctic explorer. Third in command and lieutenant-general of the expedition was Christopher Carleill, responsible for land forces totaling 1,600 soldiers. These three accomplished officers now commanded the largest fleet England had ever sent into American waters.

All told, Drake had at his disposal 2,300 men and the finest fighting ships available. As an added bonus, he was not required to carry along the many nobles and gentleman that generally accompanied such expeditions. For the most part, Drake's officers and men were veteran professionals, and it was doubtful that he would encounter the same discord that hindered him during his voyage to the Pacific. He was determined there would be no Thomas Doughtys this time around.

FRANCIS DRAKE   ECHOES OF THE DRAGON'S DRUM

Angus Konstram explains the mission that lay before Drake and his deputies:

"Drake already had his official instructions, and he had been fully briefed on the need to go through the motions of demanding redress from the Spanish. He also realized that this was little more than a diplomatic nicety. His real objective was the Spanish Main, where it was expected that he would raid the Spanish colonies, disrupt their trade and ideally intercept the annual treasure flota. For once he had the ships and men he needed to tackle this powerful Spanish force head-on. Sir Francis Walsingham—Elizabeth's foreign policy advisor and 'spymaster'—told Drake that he hoped the hardest possible blow would be struck by him.

"This voyage was therefore seen by Walsingham as a pre-emptive rather than a diplomatic measure, aimed at depriving the Spanish King of the wherewithal to wage a naval war against England. It was up to Drake how he would carry this out. After all, he knew the Caribbean like few other Englishmen, and he had spent years studying Spanish strengths and weaknesses in the New World. Drake was one of the few men who could fulfill these political objectives while satisfying the expedition's shareholders at the same time. This said, as September drew to a close Drake was eager to sail. His dread would be a last-minute recall, as the Queen had second thoughts about launching this risky strike against the Spanish New World. In the end, Drake would sooner sail before all his preparations were ready than miss the chance to continue his own private war against the Spanish, this time with the resources he needed to inflict a telling blow against his enemies."[74]

FRANCIS DRAKE — ECHOES OF THE DRAGON'S DRUM

On November 11, 1585, Drake's fleet made its first attack on a Spanish town before it even crossed the Atlantic. Five years earlier the relatively poor archipelago of the Cape Verde Islands had changed hands from the Portuguese to the Spanish. Now its capital, the small port city of Santiago, became the test site for Drake to demonstrate tactics that would prove successful time and again when his fleet later reached the Caribbean—a naval demonstration from off shore as an assault force moved into position to launch a surprise attack from land.

Since Drake's orders explicitly directed him to sail to the Caribbean and attack Spanish settlements there, historians speculate on why he chose the little Cape Verde Islands as the launching pad for the most important mission of his career. Ships sailing to the Americas did often sail south off the coast of Africa in order to catch prevailing winds, and Drake later told associates he chose the Cape Verde Islands for that purpose. However, a more direct course involved the Canary Islands instead. Theories suggest that Drake may have picked this launching point because he needed further provisions since he ordered the fleet to leave England prematurely or because he was attempting to divert the Spanish from his intended target. Neither of these theories satisfactorily tells us why Drake risked time, resources, and the lives of his men on a target that promised very little in the way of plunder.

The most likely reason for Drake's choice of the Cape Verde Islands was revenge. Three years before the expedition, William Hawkins, the father of John, had visited the islands on a peaceful trading voyage. Two of Hawkins's seven ships belonged to Drake and his brothers. Ignoring Hawkins's peaceful intentions, the Spanish garrison at Santiago launched

FRANCIS DRAKE   ECHOES OF THE DRAGON'S DRUM

a surprise attack against the anchored English ships, killing several English crew members before Hawkins could escape to safety. Much of Drake's tenacity in tracking down Spanish treasure throughout his life had been fueled by what he saw as a righteous desire for retribution. Now, as he embarked on the most important mission of his life, he could not ignore a humiliation so reminiscent of San Juan de Ulúa. Thomas Cates, the Elizabethan chronicler, later claimed that Drake attacked Santiago for the "fresh remembrance of the great wrong they had done to old Mr. William Hawkins of Plymouth, in the voyage he made four or five years before, when they did both break their promise, and murdered many of his men."[75]

Drake's attack on Santiago spotlights one of his enduring character traits. He may have been in service of the Queen, but much of his life involved fighting a very private war. From the time vengeful Catholics drove his family from their pastoral way of life until now, Drake took what he saw as Spanish arrogance and hostility personally. Before, he had been forced to overcome all odds with relatively meager resources, but now he had at his disposal the largest war fleet England had ever dared send to the Americas. He was not going to let the opportunity go unanswered.

In Santiago, Drake gained some plunder and suffered minimal losses with only one fatality among his crew. However, as the Cape Verde Islands faded from sight, an enemy against which none could defend struck the fleet. Somehow, the men of many of the ships had become infected with a lethal strain of fever. From descriptions in various ships' logs of the disease's symptoms, the likely culprit was some form of

FRANCIS DRAKE — ECHOES OF THE DRAGON'S DRUM

typhus. Next to scurvy, typhus, often called "jail fever," was the most common affliction that struck mariners on long voyages. Unlike scurvy, however, typhus had no known cure and took as many lives as it spared. The word typhus means "hazy." The severe fever caused by the disease often left sufferers that survived so addled they were of little use sailing a ship or fighting battles. The first appearance of typhus occurred barely one hundred years earlier during the Spanish siege of Moorish Grenada, and it is certain Drake and his men knew the story well. Who could forget the tales of fever, red blotches, delirium, rotting flesh, and death? During that one siege, 3,000 Spaniards fell to enemy action, but 17,000 succumbed to jail fever and perished.

This could not have been a worse beginning for an expedition that had so much riding on its success. Like prisons, ships of the time provided a perfect breeding ground for typhus with their crowded, unsanitary conditions. The crew of the *Elizabeth Bonaventure*, the largest ship of the fleet, suffered most. Within days, the majority of her crew agonized with fever and worse. In two weeks' time, nearly a hundred were dead. Things were not much better on the other ships. The *Primrose* recorded sixty dead, and before the fleet reached the West Indies, a total of 300 English seamen and soldiers had been consigned to the depths of the sea. Two of Drake's primary attack ships had lost one-third of their crews. The survivors, feeble and debilitated, were in no condition to take part in an assault on a defended city. Those not stricken or not severely ill had a full month of sailing to recover.

On New Year's Day, 1586, Drake's fleet arrived at the Spanish Main and set to besieging Santo Domingo. Once again, captured ships yielded

FRANCIS DRAKE   ECHOES OF THE DRAGON'S DRUM

only meager amounts of gold and silver, so Drake blockaded the city to negotiate a ransom. By mid-January, Drake reached a settlement with the Spanish negotiator, Garcia Fernandez de Torrequemada. The city agreed to pay Drake a tribute of 50,000 pesos, far less than he hoped for, but time was of the essence so Drake accepted the ransom. In exchange, Drake promised to spare what remained of the town and to sail away once the ransom was paid. In his report to the king, Torrequemada included his assessment of Drake:

> *"Francis Drake knows no language but English, and I talked with him through interpreters in Latin or French or Italian. He had with him an Englishman who understood a little Spanish, and who sometimes acted as interpreter. Drake is a man of medium stature, fair-haired, heavy rather than slender and jovial yet careful. He commands and rules imperiously, and is feared and obeyed by his men. He punishes resolutely. He is sharp, restless, well-spoken, inclined to liberality and to ambition, vain, boastful, and not notably cruel. These are the qualities I saw in him during my negotiations."*[76]

The phrase "not notably cruel" spoke volumes. The Spanish were notably cruel throughout the Americas at this time. While El Draco spread fear throughout the area, he remained known as a surprisingly fair man prone to pardon rather than vengeance. But he had his limits as Santo Domingo soon discovered. During the negotiations, Drake sent a delegation to the Spanish camp with a message. The party included a black boy who had recently joined Drake's force following the capture of the city. Even though the party approached under a flag of truce, one of the Spaniards stabbed and mortally wounded the boy, possibly because he recognized

FRANCIS DRAKE ECHOES OF THE DRAGON'S DRUM

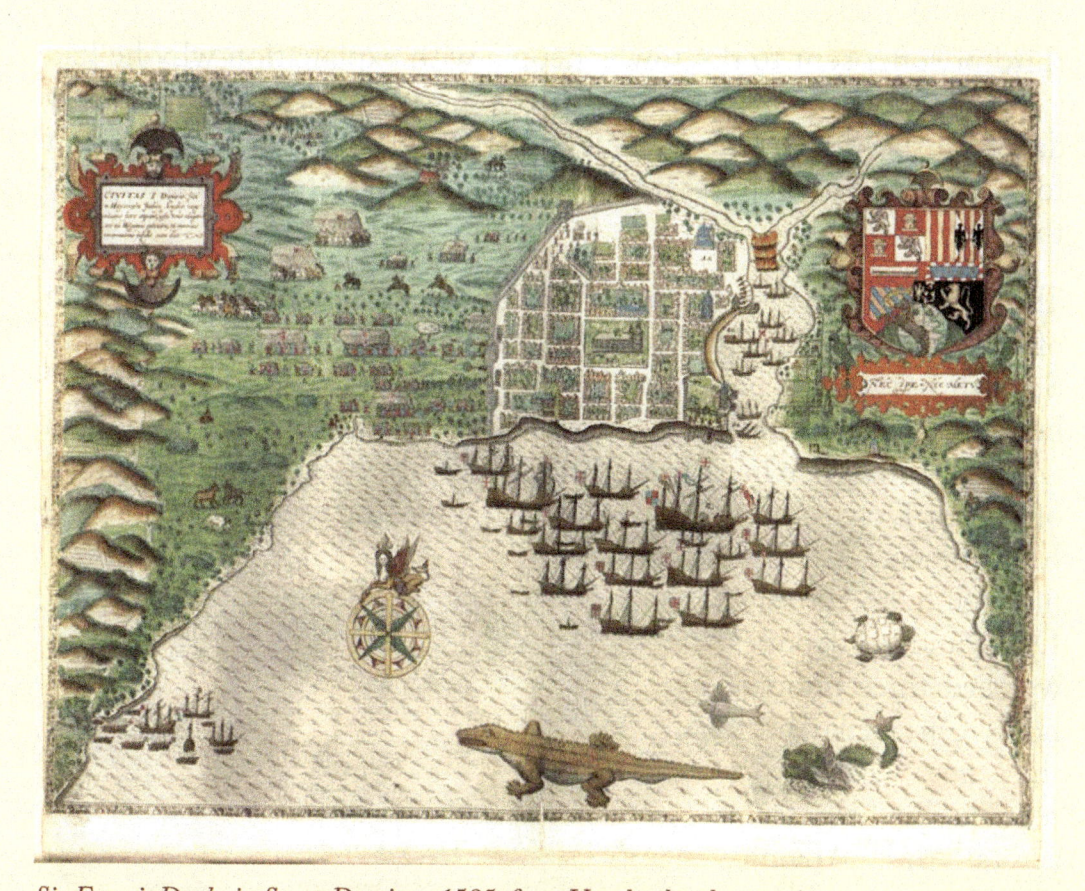

Sir Francis Drake in Santo Domingo 1585, from Hand-colored engraving, by Baptista Boazio, 1589.

him as a runaway slave. The party took the boy back to the city where he died before Drake's very eyes in the cathedral. The commander was furious in a way many said they never saw before or after in their leader. Drake responded to the treachery by ordering a gallows built for all in the city to see. Two captured Dominican friars were then brought out and hanged in full view of their shocked countrymen. Drake ordered a

FRANCIS DRAKE   ECHOES OF THE DRAGON'S DRUM

third prisoner sent to the towns people with explanation why he had executed the priests. He promised to hang two more prisoners every day until the culprit was punished. The Spanish had little choice but to comply, and the murderer was accordingly executed within sight of the city.

Throughout late winter and early spring, Drake continued this pattern of capturing any ships that got in his way and dealing the same fate to Spanish port towns he had to Santo Domingo. Four major ports fell before the unrelenting raids in which Drake's men burned and looted with impunity. Then in early April 1587 another disease forced a council of war for Drake and his captains. Malaria now turned its sights on the Englishmen. As their men fell by the dozens, Drake and his deputies weighed three options: hold Cartagena until the fleet could be relieved by help from across the Atlantic, commence a raid on another port city, or return to England.

Francis Drake in St. Augustine.

Dudley observes: "Sir Francis alone had to weigh the factors and decide on the final

FRANCIS DRAKE   ECHOES OF THE DRAGON'S DRUM

course for the expedition. What with local prostitutes, individual looting, and sheer boredom, discipline among these men showed signs of rapid deterioration; Drake had been forced to hang several men as examples. Reluctantly, the admiral decided to accept the relatively small ransom finally gathered by the local governor and to begin the voyage home."[77]

By mid-April, after pausing for water and provisions in Cuba, Drake led the fleet up the coast of Florida, only pausing to sack the Spanish town of Saint Augustine. From there Drake continued northward to the English colony of Roanoke recently established by Sir Walter Raleigh and Sir Richard Greenville. The colony's supply ship had failed to arrive, so the colonists joined Drake's fleet on its voyage back to England.[78] The time had come to go home.

On 27 July 1586, Drake and what remained of his expedition sailed into Plymouth, where cheering crowds greeted them. The great expedition had lasted ten months and effectively singed the beard of King Philip. 2,600 men and boys had waved goodbye to friends and family less than a year earlier, but only 700 returned. Such campaigns always had a higher cost than gold and silver. Drake managed to obtain a reasonable amount of plunder and shatter the illusion that Spain was invincible. He and his men pillaged four Spanish settlements with ease and confirmed the vulnerability of the Spanish empire in the New World. Even more importantly, with war imminent, the English now believed they could take on the might of Spain and win.

Drake's expedition did not prove wildly successful as a financial enterprise, and this caused him problems for months to come. All the investors, including Queen Elizabeth, received an initial return on their investment of just 75 per cent. As always, there were accusations of pilfering and outright theft on all sides. On other voyages, this might have caused both Drake and the Queen concern, but there had been one definite bonanza that was irrefutable—Spain had been hit hard and the political fortune was immense.

Lord Burghley saw that the raid had proved a major humiliation for the Spanish. He put this simply in a letter to the Queen by declaring, "Sir Francis Drake is a man fearful to the King of Spain."[79] Burghley was right. Drake had captured two key cities, Cartagena and Santo Domingo, on the Spanish Main. By doing so, he demonstrated to the international powers the fragility of King Philip's empire. Spain's creditors understood the message Drake sent to Spain; within months of the fleet's return, those creditors turned down King Philip's request for a loan of 500,000 ducats. As rumors spread throughout Europe that the Spanish could not protect their annual shipments of treasure. The banking house in Seville collapsed. Even Pope Sixtus V acknowledged that Drake's achievements had struck a powerful political blow to Philip.

Despite Drake's recent accomplishment, what he might do next concerned Spain just as much or more. The boost to England's national morale was incalculable as she now had a legitimate national hero whose feats were swiftly becoming legendary. With the prospect of war looming, England was certain it could count on men like Sir Francis Drake to safeguard her from the fury of the Spanish. One of the ironies of history is that Queen Elizabeth was mistaken in believing Drake's mission could prevent war. Ironically, Drake's expedition forced

FRANCIS DRAKE   ECHOES OF THE DRAGON'S DRUM

King Philip to appreciate that he could only safeguard his empire by destroying Queen Elizabeth's England.

Konstam's observations about the effect of Drake's raids in the Spanish Main are appropriate:

> "With the benefit of hindsight we can see that the belief that Drake's raid would help prevent a war was incredibly naive. The idea was that it would give King Philip pause, and make him consider the consequences of an all-out war with England. Of course, Drake's raid achieved exactly the opposite. At the time King Philip was embroiled in a long and costly war against the Dutch Protestant rebels. His commander, the Duke of Parma, captured the city of Antwerp in August 1585, which safeguarded Spain's earlier conquests in the Spanish Netherlands. He was irritated by overt English support for the rebels, and so before launching a final offensive against the Dutch, King Philip felt he needed to deal with the English problem once and for all. That effectively meant invading England.

> "Back in Spain, King Philip's advisors argued that Drake's success would encourage others, and the seas would be filled by English privateers, all eager for a share of Spain's riches. The first of these privateers were already at sea. Only by defeating England could Spanish sea communications be protected, and the security of her overseas empire preserved. Consequently King Philip asked his leading commanders, the Duke of Santa Cruz and the Duke of Parma, to draft plans for an invasion. This set in train the events which would lead to Spain's 'Great Enterprise against England'—the Spanish Armada of 1588."[80]

M.re DE L ACADEMIE ROYALE des SCIENCES
et quelques autres et sur les memoires les plus recens
PAR M. DE L'ISLE
GROENLAND
MER GLACIALE
CANADA
GOLFE DE MEXIQUE
Detroit de Magellan

FRANCIS DRAKE — ECHOES OF THE DRAGON'S DRUM

Defeat of the Spanish Armada (1588)

Once more unto the breach, dear friends, once more;
Or close the wall up with our English dead!
In peace there's nothing so becomes a man
As modest stillness and humility:
But when the blast of war blows in our ears,
Then imitate the action of the tiger;
Stiffen the sinews, summon up the blood,
Disguise fair nature with hard favoured rage;
Then lend the eye a terrible aspect....
On, on you noblest English!
Whose blood is fet from fathers of war-proof!
Fathers that, like so many Alexanders,
Have in these parts from morn till even fought
And sheathed their swords for lack of argument....
And you, good yeomen,
Whose limbs were made in England, show us here
The mettle of your pasture....
I see you stand like greyhounds in the slips,
Straining upon the start. The game's afoot:
Follow your spirit, and upon this charge
Cry "God for Harry, England, and Saint George!"

—William Shakespeare

FRANCIS DRAKE   ECHOES OF THE DRAGON'S DRUM

Even before Sir Francis Drake returned from his raids on the Spanish Main, England and Spain were racing headlong on a collision course toward war. At the center of things was Elizabeth's cousin, Mary Stuart—Mary, Queen of Scots—whom Elizabeth had under lock and key. Up until now, Elizabeth had deferred to the conventions of her day that protected monarchs, regardless of their complicity, from capital punishment. One major factor led her to change her mind. Having no heir, Elizabeth and her court worried who would succeed to the throne should she die. Drake was one among many in England who carried vivid memories of the Counter-Reformation and Mary Tudor's brief but bloody time on the throne as a Roman Catholic queen. No Protestant cared to face what would certainly occur if Mary Stuart, ever managed to gain release from her imprisonment. Then in July of 1586, Drake's old ally, Walsingham, uncovered a Catholic plot against Elizabeth's life that directly implicated Mary. Mary paid for her part in the plot with her in life on the axe-man's block at Fotheringay Castle in February the following year.

With his mother out of the way, Mary's son James became the undisputed heir to the throne, and he seemed a committed Calvinist. Both Francis Drake's bold raids in the New World and Mary's death made it almost certain that Philip would unleash his mighty Armada against England. As long as Mary lived, Philip doubted the wisdom of overthrowing Elizabeth. Though he considered her a heretic, Elizabeth actually presented fewer political complications than Mary. The restoration of Catholicism would put Mary on the throne and, with her blood ties to the French, England and France might become committed allies. Philip wanted none of that. Rather, he envisioned himself the legitimate

FRANCIS DRAKE — ECHOES OF THE DRAGON'S DRUM

Catholic heir to Elizabeth's crown by virtue of his marriage to Mary I, the last Roman Catholic Tudor. His Armada would simply be restoring the rightful religion and rightful king of England.

Speaking of the inevitable nature of a Spanish invasion and the political nightmare faced by Queen Elizabeth, Sugden writes:

> *"None saw that coming Armada more clearly than Francis Drake. Few were so reluctant to see it as Elizabeth. How different they were, the aggressive, fiery zealot and the cautious, war-weary monarch. For Drake life was approaching its climax, the ultimate contest for which he had been preparing all these years—a decisive clash of armour not just between England and Spain but also between God and Antichrist. Far from shrinking from it, he thirsted for the action, supremely self-confident, guided by temperament as well as logic to the opinion that Elizabeth must strike first, disorient her enemies and disrupt their preparations. No sooner was he home than he was canvassing for another expedition.*

> *"Elizabeth listened to Drake because she recognized his unswerving loyalty and understood his value, and perhaps because she often found his hearty and frank conversation entertaining. But every time she saw the burly little seaman swaggering forward she knew what he was going to say. He wanted money, ships and men to hit Philip hard. Strike Spain now, before the Armada could sail! His message was always the same, and there were always those, like Walsingham and Leicester, who would echo it.*

> *"And yet she feared to let them have their way. She could not comprehend*

FRANCIS DRAKE — ECHOES OF THE DRAGON'S DRUM

the depth of their hostility to Spain and the Pope, and she took a broader view of the international scene. To her it was not purely a matter of Spain and England. She could not forget that France was her closest neighbour and had long been her rival. How would it serve England to destroy Spain, the one country capable of curbing the power of France? Not only that but a war, any war, would fracture her hard-won and fragile solvency. She had only to review the annals of her father's reign to learn how money squandered on foreign adventures could beggar the Exchequer. Despite the legacy of her extravagant forbears she had paid her debts, revalued the debased coinage and created a reserve fund, but with a gross income of less than half a million pounds a year her government was already in trouble again. Everybody wanted money. Drake wanted it for ships. Leicester wanted it for his Netherlands army, although it had performed little and had exceeded its allocated budget of £126,000 a year. The Dutch wanted money, and so did the French Huguenots. With chagrin Elizabeth saw her chested reserve fall by four-fifths between 1584 and 1588 to a mere £55,000, less than it would take for the full mobilization of her fleet. She had looked for dividends from Drake, but however successful his raid of the West Indies had been militarily it had failed her financially. There was an alternative, one she should have taken, but she hated to use it. She could ask Parliament to raise taxes. Elizabeth's perennial stringency reflected less a lack of wealth than a reluctance to tap it. The propertied escaped lightly under her regime. Her take from the national income may have been as low as three per cent and custom rates remained low. This was one reason why so many merchants were able to sink funds into privateering. The queen's reluctance to tax more heavily was, in the light

FRANCIS DRAKE — ECHOES OF THE DRAGON'S DRUM

of growing national danger, probably irresponsible but not unreasoned. Taxation caused unrest, and it increased Elizabeth's dependence upon Parliament, which alone had the right to grant it. She resisted putting herself in the hands of those whose judgment she distrusted. And she resisted a more oppressive taxation. So she prevaricated and stalled while the storm brewed about her, grasping the flimsiest straws to preserve peace, clinging to hope after it had gone. Drake and Elizabeth were bound by a common patriotism, but they exasperated each other whenever they discussed policy."[81]

One of Drake's overriding character traits was his knack for pressing an issue while others debated it. Drake's early victories in the Spanish Main resulted from his refusal to hesitate and his dogged pursuit of a goal. When faced with disappointing results tracking Spanish treasure ships, he regrouped and devised a way to intercept the treasure on land by taking Spain's mule train. Though older and slowing a bit, Francis Drake was still not one to sit and wait for opportunity. Elizabeth, on the other hand, had a decided bent toward caution that frustrated her aggressive Sea Dog on numerous occasions. For months after his return from the Spanish Main, Drake petitioned the Queen repeatedly to allow him to strike the brand while hot and hit Spain on her own soil.

Elizabeth, hoping to avoid outright war, continued to deflect Drake's requests and ultimately dispatched him to the Netherlands as her emissary. However, Drake was no diplomat, so he soon returned to the Queen's court still begging for permission to strike Spanish ports before the Spanish completed their preparations for war. Elizabeth continued

FRANCIS DRAKE   ECHOES OF THE DRAGON'S DRUM

to waver until, in March 1587, she relented to pressure from key advisors like Chancellor Walsingham. On his advice, she ordered Drake to harass the Armada within its ports, interdict coastal shipping, and, if feasible, take Spanish treasure ships. Within days of receiving his orders and without wasting time to ensure full provisioning, he led his fleet from Plymouth harbor bound for Spanish port cities. Francis Drake loved and respected his Queen, but he also knew her. She had ordered what he had always believed must be done, and he was not going to offer any time for her to change her mind. His last message to Walsingham read: "The wind commands me away. Our ship's under sail. God grant we may live in His fear as the enemy may have cause to say that God doth fight for Her Majesty as well abroad as at home. . . . Haste!"[82]

Drake's decision to make haste leaving Plymouth proved wise. Not long after the ships of his expedition passed the horizon, a royal messenger appeared in Plymouth delivering orders that would have limited Drake's mission. Aboard a fast-sailing pinnace, the messenger attempted, but failed to catch up to Drake's command ship. Some historians have speculated that the messenger's ship failed to reach Drake because of a storm, but one of the younger sons of the Hawkin's family captained the pinnace. The Hawkins clan's hatred for Spain matched that of Drake, and none of them would have cared to exert much effort in stopping their cousin from accomplishing his mission.

Sir Francis commanded sixteen ships and three thousand sailors and soldiers from the deck of the *Elizabeth Bonaventure*. As usual, various investors, including the Queen, funded the expedition. As had occurred so often before, the sea nearly ended Drake's enterprise before it began.

FRANCIS DRAKE — ECHOES OF THE DRAGON'S DRUM

Within a day of leaving England, a storm engulfed the fleet in winds and driving rain for four days. With his attack fleet scattered, Drake waited at Lisbon and prayed. Apparently those prayers were answered because only one small pinnace didn't make the rendezvous point in Lisbon. The next day, Drake captured a Portuguese pinnace that carried no gold, but instead yielded a far greater prize—intelligence. Now he knew what his first target must be. Cádiz held a substantial concentration of shipping, including galleons of the Armada, local merchantmen, and supply vessels. When Drake learned the garrison commander had no idea his port was in jeopardy, he knew it was time to attack.

A perceived strength can also be a weakness as Drake learned all too often when it came to the Royal navy tradition of war councils. He was man of impulse and daring, able to discern almost by instinct where and how to hit the enemy next. However, a council of war required conferring with other captains of more measured dispositions. Borough suggested caution: observe and assess the defenses of Cádiz before planning an attack. To his credit, Drake listened as he had seldom done before. But the voice that spoke the loudest was the one that came from within. Decades of raiding had schooled Drake in the value of unexpected and sudden assault. At the end of the council Drake ordered the fleet to set sail for Cádiz, but Borough demanded specific instructions. The reply probably left the vice-admiral shaking his head. His admiral simply said, "Follow me."

Spain proved ill prepared for Drake's lightning attacks first on the port of Cádiz and later on Corunna. He summarily overwhelmed the naval vessels assigned to protecting the ports and occupied their harbors.

FRANCIS DRAKE   ECHOES OF THE DRAGON'S DRUM

During these raids, the English fleet captured 35 merchant and military vessels setting Philip's timeline for attacking England back by at least a year. Over the next month, Drake continued his assault on the coast of Spain, destroying scores of ships and thoroughly disrupting supply lines. Only one incident blemished the fleet's rousing success. Borough, who had sent a communiqué to Drake challenging him for leadership of the fleet, required discipline. As the campaign wound to an end, Drake ordered his vice-admiral stripped of rank and confined to his cabin to await trial in England for his cowardice. Either the Dragon did not understand the political realities of Elizabeth's court, or more likely, did not care. Boroughs was a court favorite, but Drake had learned the danger of hesitation in dealing with insubordination with Thomas Doughty. For Drake, the immediate mattered far more than any potential future ramifications for his decisions.

The mission was an unmitigated success and when Drake returned to England, the Queen made him vice-admiral, serving under Lord Howard of Effingham. During his return from Spain, Drake wrote: "it hath pleased God that we have taken forts, ships, barks, carvels, and divers other vessels more than a hundred, most laden, some with oars for galleys, planks and timber for ships and pinnaces, hoops and pipe-staves for cask, with many other provisions for this great army."[83] Sir Francis Drake had positioned himself to assume a major role in the most famous battle in English history.

On July 12, 1588, Philip's legendary Armada entered the English Channel. Henry VIII's "Broad Ditch" remained the last barrier protecting the English Reformation and Elizabeth's reign, and by most

FRANCIS DRAKE   ECHOES OF THE DRAGON'S DRUM

estimations there was no way it could offer much protection now. Philip's plan was simple: conquer and depose the Protestant Elizabeth, establish himself as monarch, and return England to the Roman Catholic fold. His Armada appeared invincible. It included 150 ships, 8,000 sailors, 18,000 soldiers, and enough cannon to sink anything English that got in its way. The fleet was so immense that it had taken two full days to clear Spanish ports.

From the pope to the least pauper in Spain, the power and might of the Armada seemed so great that it was generally known as La Armada Invencible. The Duke of Medina Sidonia, chosen to lead the fleet referred to his command as La Felicisima Armada—the blessed fleet. However, it appeared the new commander harbored doubts as to fleet's readiness. He spoke bluntly to King Philip: "To undertake so great a task with equal forces to those of the enemy would be inadvisable, but to do so with an inferior force, as ours is now, with our men lacking in experience, would be still more unwise. I am bound to confess that I see very few, or hardly any, of those on the armada with any knowledge of or ability to perform the duties entrusted to them. I have tested and watched this point very carefully, and your Majesty may believe me when I assure you that we are very weak."[84] Unlike Elizabeth, Philip seldom listened to his advisors and before long, he discovered his fleet, though mighty, was far from invincible.

The Queen selected a fleet admiral, Lord Charles Howard of Effingham, to lead England's ships against the Armada. Though Sir Francis Drake may seem like the logical choice for admiral considering his string of resounding victories, his handling of Borough likely prevented that.

FRANCIS DRAKE — ECHOES OF THE DRAGON'S DRUM

The Queen found Borough innocent of wrongdoing (after taking into account the false testimony of his crew and his political connections). In fairness, however, it is also reasonable to believe that Elizabeth knew Howard would take a more measured approach and felt Drake's privateer's heart ill-suited for leading the defense of England against the Armada. Thus, Howard became lord admiral with Drake his vice-admiral. Happily, they worked together in deferential harmony.

As the Spanish Armada proceeded with its assault on the Channel, it did indeed appear invincible. Then, on July 21, the winds shifted in a turn of events known to every English schoolchild for centuries to come. With the Spanish ships somewhat scattered, Howard seized the advantage as he divided his forces between himself and Drake. The English set a number of Spanish ships afire. Then Howard called a council aboard the flagship. To Drake he assigned the honor of leading the pursuit as the struggling Armada sought to reassemble. Drake's orders were to keep a lantern burning at the stern of his ship to serve as a beacon to lead rest of the fleet through the darkness. It is at this point that Drake's privateering ways caused problems. During pursuit of the Armada, Drake ship came upon the damaged *Rosario* and accepted its surrender the following morning. Why he failed to pursue the bulk of the Armada and, more importantly, why he extinguished his stern light is still a matter of debate. When Admiral Howard confronted his vice-admiral, Drake gave the excuse that he had paused to investigate a strange sail, only to stumble upon the disabled Spanish. No justifiable reason for failing to light the way for other English ships was ever given.

In spite of Drake's momentary diversion, he quickly rejoined the fleet

FRANCIS DRAKE ECHOES OF THE DRAGON'S DRUM

to engage the enemy. The sun rose on July 22 to reveal an Armada in total disarray. Leading the assault, Drake's squadron inflicted the most damage. The battle raged for nine hours leaving three of Medina Sidonia's most powerful ships either sunk or beached. Two days later, what remained of the mighty Armada had no choice but to withdraw. It came none too soon since Howard's men were dying by the dozens from scurvy and fever.

Summing up the victory in the English Channel, Dudley writes:

> "La Invencible Armada would never return to trouble the waters of the Channel. Only sixty of the Catholic horde survived the expedition—the wreckage of the remainder still rests along the shores of Scotland and Ireland. In England, Elizabeth and her people gave thanks to their Protestant God for his mercy, and praised the many brave men who had defeated the Spanish abomination. But in Spain, and throughout Catholic Europe, one man's name remained tied to the defeat of the Armada—El Draque. That Protestant devil had breathed his flames upon the harbor of Calais, and Philip's Great Endeavor had crumbled before it. However, as those who had looked in vain for Drake's lantern knew, it was perhaps too much credit for a man who had fought for his God and fought for his queen—until he saw the opportunity for plunder."[85]

DE L'ACADEMIE ROYALE des SCIENCES
et quelques autres et sur les memoires les plus recens
PAR M. DE L'ISLE
CANADA
MEXIQUE
GOLFE DE MEXIQUE
Antarctique

Francis Drake — Echoes of the Dragon's Drum

And With the Imminent Danger Passed (1589)

She stood atop the ridge with soulful eyes
attuned to sunsets far away,
beyond the stretch of darkened woods
that held her heart at bay.

The proud armada danced upon the waves,
yet still her mien was harsh and cold;
no words could frame her angled chin
and marble stance so bold.

War took her heart into a distant mist,
where cruel time might seal its fate—
to England! Now, as daggered light
made future darkness wait.

—Rich Roach

Francis Drake returned from both his circumnavigation of the world and his second expedition to the Spanish Main a national hero. Like no other of his time, he had captured the imagination of a people desperately in need of one. Though still a public icon, the ending of the war with Spain in 1588 came like the slow trickle of a leaking faucet. This time Elizabeth did not ask him to conquer worlds, but rather to

FRANCIS DRAKE   ECHOES OF THE DRAGON'S DRUM

tackle the tedious business of tying up loose ends, many of which were complicated and frayed. On shore, thousands of beleaguered sailors and soldiers returned from months of patrol and open warfare at sea still fighting against scurvy and disease or their aftereffects. To make matters worse, Elizabeth and her privy council welcomed those who had just saved their country with weeks and weeks of excuses for delayed medical treatment and pay. With the imminent threat of what had once been thought an invincible Armada gone, there also was now time for accusations and recriminations that continued for months.

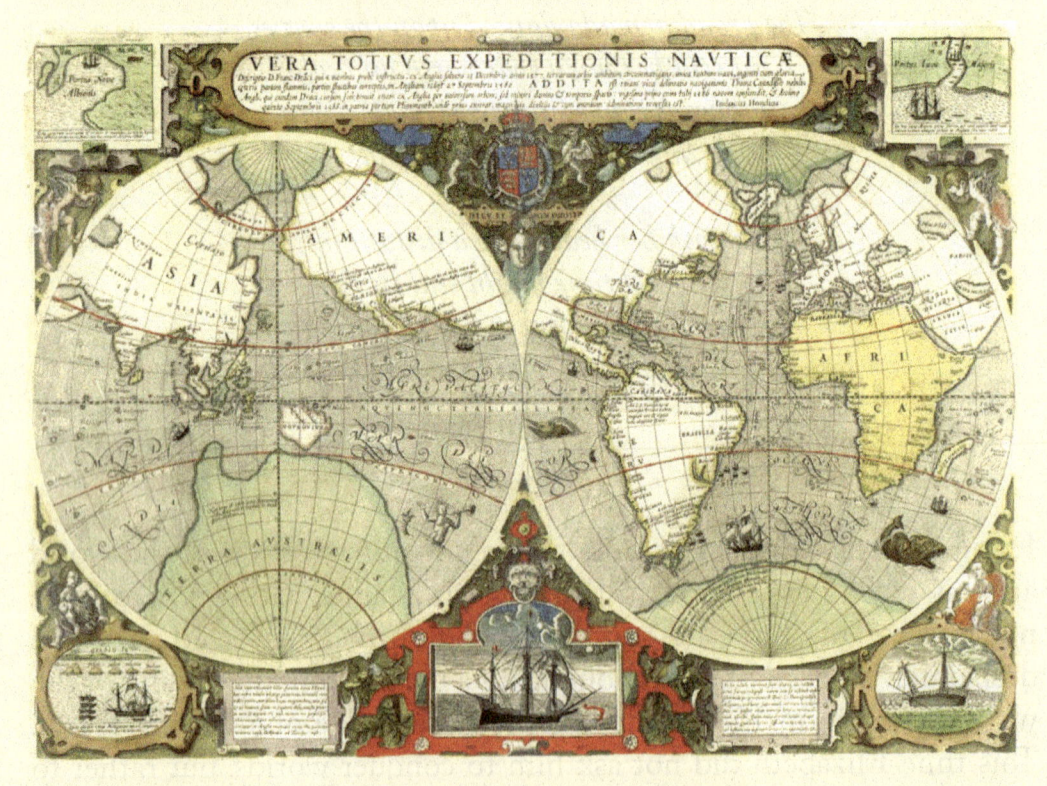

Vera Totius Expeditionis Nauticae showing route of Francis Drake's Circumnavigation of the globe.

FRANCIS DRAKE — ECHOES OF THE DRAGON'S DRUM

A man of action like Drake probably was grateful to escape the drama as the Queen assigned him and Sir John Norreys, the duty of patrolling the shores of England and Spain to destroy whatever remaining Spanish ships they could. Sadly, this final mission of the war was a disaster. The English fleet managed to capture a few ships at La Coruna, but paid a high price in ships and lives for the effort. Together, Drake and Norreys lost 12,000 men and 20 war ships with little to show in return.

When the campaign proved futile, Elizabeth then sent Drake and Norreys off to capture the Azores, hoping to strengthen England's position against Spain should she be able to make Portugal an ally. Again, the mission was doomed to failure before it began. After many years enjoying his standing as Elizabeth's "pirate," Francis found himself past middle age and ignored by the Queen. Military men may win every conflict on the field or sea of battle, but still fall victim to hopeless political skirmishes at home.

Some biographers have portrayed Drake's last years as a time of failure and disfavor. Several years did pass in which he spent most of his time with his wife at their Abbey. He pursued business interests and other matters, but never lost affection for his first mistress, the sea. Though pushed aside for a season by the realities of court life, he was not finished yet. Dudley writes of this period of Drake's life:

> "Perhaps some measure of good luck did remain; at least Sir Francis retained his title and his personal wealth—as well as his head. However, Elizabeth no longer sought his advice or welcomed him at court. Some men would have remained in London, hoping for a reprieve from the

FRANCIS DRAKE — ECHOES OF THE DRAGON'S DRUM

queen. Others would have retired to their country homes to live their remaining years in peace. Sir Francis did neither; instead he remained active in the local life at Plymouth. Fearing a Spanish invasion, the town sought his help in putting the local defenses in order. Then, as the war with Spain continued, the queen's council named Drake as a prize commissioner for Plymouth. It was an interesting choice, placing an aging but unreformed pirate in charge of providing an inventory of prize goods."[86]

Along the way, Drake slowly found himself again in the good graces of his Queen. Much of the reason for this turn of events was the old Sea Dog's longevity. The sun was setting on the age of the English privateers, and few able to fight remained. Drake's chief advocate in court, Walsingham, died in 1590, and not long after, Sir Richard Green perished along with Drake's old flagship, the *Revenge*. However, the man who helped launch his career, John Hawkins, still sailed, and together they approached Elizabeth about a joint mission to the West Indies. Still desperate for capital, the Queen agreed to one last mission.

A Fitting Place to Die (1596)

*England, his heart; his corpse the waters have;
And that which raised his fame became his grave.*

—Richard Barnfield,

It isn't that life ashore is distasteful to me. But life at sea is better.

—Francis Drake

Drake's *Defiance* and Hawkins's *Garland* set sail in August of 1595 with the expedition's sights set on a damaged treasure ship rumored to be moored in Puerto Rico. Hawkins and Drake were at odds not days after the ships sailed, which may have been prophetic of what lay ahead. Even more foreboding is the fact Drake took one thing along with him he never had before—his will. Thomas Maynarde, who knew both Sea Dogs well, wrote a few years later about this last voyage:

"Sir Francis Drake . . . a man of great spirit and fit to undertake matters. In my poor opinion better able to conduct forces and discreetly to govern in conducting them to places where service was to be done, than to command in the execution thereof. But assuredly his very name was a great terror to the enemy in all those parts, having heretofore done many things . . . to his honourable fame and profit. But entering into them as the child of fortune, it may be his self-willed and peremptory command was doubted, and that caused Her Majesty (as should seem) to join Sir John Hawkins in equal commission, a man old and wary,

FRANCIS DRAKE   ECHOES OF THE DRAGON'S DRUM

entering into matters with so leaden a foot that the other's meat would be eaten before his spit could come to the fire, men of so different natures and dispositions that what the one desireth the other would commonly oppose against . . . whom the one loved the other smally esteemed."[87]

The Spanish had years to fortify their port cities and strengthen their defenses in the Spanish Main. On numerous occasions, Drake argued for hitting the Main while it was in disarray only to be rebuffed or delayed. Ever since the Dragon first spread his wings and rained fear down on the Spanish in Panama a quarter century earlier, he understood the key to halting Spain's design on world domination lay in the New World rather than the Old. In spite of this, he faced what many a military genius has throughout the annals of time. While he pressed for another victory before he enemy regrouped, Elizabeth and her council preferred a more measured approach. And now the Spanish proved ready for Hawkins and Drake as they sailed into San Juan Bay.

No sooner had the planned attack begun than John Hawkins, now past age 60, proved too slow and unsure to fight. On November 12, 1595, the second greatest of Elizabeth's Sea Dogs lay dead near San Juan. The two cousins had lived through both exciting and tumultuous times. Both were able seaman, but close associates never doubted it was the younger of the two who remained the greatest of the Sea Dogs. A close contemporary known only as RM wrote in his journal comparing Hawkins and Drake:

"They were both of many virtues, and agreeing in some. As patience in enduring labours and hardness, observation and memory of things

FRANCIS DRAKE   ECHOES OF THE DRAGON'S DRUM

past, and great discretion in sudden dangers in which neither of them [were] much distempered; and in some other virtues they differed. Sir John Hawkins had in him mercy and aptness to forgive, and true of word; Sir Francis hard in reconciliation and constancy in friendship; he was withal severe and courteous, magnanimous, and liberal. They were both faulty in ambition, but more the one than the other; for in Sir Francis was an insatiable desire of honour, indeed beyond reason. He was infinite in promises, and more temperate in adversity than in better fortune. He had also other imperfections, as aptness to anger, and bitterness in disgracing, and too much pleased with open flattery. Sir John Hawkins had in him malice with dissimulation, rudeness in behaviour and passing sparing [tight-fisted], indeed miserable. They were both happy alike in being great commanders and grew great and famous by one means, rising through their own virtues and the fortune of the sea. [But] there was no comparison to be made between their well-deserving and good parts, for therein Sir Francis Drake did far exceed."[88]

Now there was just Francis Drake to carry on. The expedition aimed for Panama with hopes of recovering something of its losses before returning home, but morale was low. "The men," writes Sugden, "had seen Francis Drake rebuffed twice now, at Grand Canary and San Juan, and inevitably their concern was mounting, especially in those whose pay depended upon the plunder taken. To mariners who had sailed under the admiral's flag in better times it was increasingly obvious that Sit Francis was at the bottom of his form. He was not the man he had once been."[89]

FRANCIS DRAKE — ECHOES OF THE DRAGON'S DRUM

After a few successes, in a touch of tragic irony, Drake reached Nombre de Dios two days after Christmas. He had come full circle to the scene of his first great triumph, and it was here the Dragon could find no more fire to spew on the city. He had come here early in his career with a single ship and a handful of his fellow Devon seamen to strike fear into the hearts of the proud Spanish. Now he arrived with a powerful force to a town all but deserted. Warned in advance, only a small garrison remained, and there would be miles of travel up the River Charges to find the escaped treasure. Drake ordered a contingent to pursue, but it met stiff opposition and most were killed.

Drake, always an optimist, desperately struggled to find something positive to present to his men. Resources were now running low and so was Drake's ability to put a good face on the situation. Over the next two weeks, a depression fell over the commander like few who knew him had ever seen. Thomas Maynarde writing at the time said:

"He answered me with grief, protesting that he was as ignorant of the Indies as myself, and that he never thought any place could be so changed, as it were from a delicious and pleasant arbour into a waste and desert wilderness, besides the variableness of the wind and weather, so stormy and blusterous as he never saw it before. But he most wondered that since his coming out of England he never saw sail worthy the giving chase unto. Yet in the greatness of his mind, he would in the end conclude with these words: 'It matters not, man; God hath many things in store for us, and I know many means to do Her Majesty good service and to make us rich, for we must have gold before we see England.'"[90]

FRANCIS DRAKE — ECHOES OF THE DRAGON'S DRUM

Soon it became obvious to all that Francis Drake was not well and probably would not recover. The crew of the *Defiance* noticed how their captain stayed below in his cabin and was seen only by his servants and senior officers. As the fleet reached Buena Ventura, sickness took one victim after another. Both Captain Josias of the *Defiance* and the fleet surgeon James Wood lay dead and Drake had not moved from his cabin in weeks. In his last few days, Drake valiantly fought to remain of sound mind as he could see troubles already brewing over his estate. Near morning, on January 28, Sir Francis Drake grew delirious. A proud Sea Dog to the end, he rose from his bed and called for his servant to help him dress and buckle his armor, but his aide persuaded Drake to return to his bed. A crewman onboard the *Defiance* wrote in his diary:

> "The 28th at four of the clock in the morning our General, Sir Francis Drake departed this life, having been extremely sick of a flux, which began the night before to stop on him. He used some speeches at, or a little before, his death, rising and appareling himself, but being brought to bed again within one hour died. He made his brother Thomas Drake and captain Jonas Bodenham executors, and M. Thomas Drake's son his heir to all his lands except one manor which he gave to Captain Bodenham.

> "The same day we anchored at Puerto Bello, being the best harbor we found along the main both for great ships and small..."[91]

With the fleet anchored at Puerto Bello, a sermon was preached aboard the *Defiance*; then the captains and principal officers gave their beloved General, now encased in a lead coffin, back to the sea.

Mrs de l'Academie Royale des Sciences
et quelques autres et sur les memoires les plus recens
Par M. de L'Isle

Conclusion

There must be a beginning of any great matter, but the continuing unto the end until it be thoroughly finished yields the true glory.

—Sir Francis Drake

The more than 400 years since Francis Drake's death have seen his memory ride waves of accolades followed by times of forgetfulness and so on. Because of his brief direct connection with slavery, some moderns have come to view Drake as nothing more than a man willing to prey on the misery of others for his own gain. Some, feeling the need to vindicate him, have exalted Drake as a man above men, a figure without fault to be revered without question. Neither view is balanced, nor does justice to what made Francis Drake such an important figure in the history of the Western World.

One Drake website has gone out of its way to offer a view of Drake akin to sainthood: "In the long history of the British nation, we have produced many brave men; skilled sailors; navigators and naval commanders; intrepid explorers, brilliant strategists, outstanding political administrators and other colourful characters. However, there has only been one Englishman who possessed all of these qualities and executed them with such panache and élan that has created an eternal legend. To emphasize this point, the novelist Georgette Heyer wrote, 'There was and is only one Drake.' For this endorsement alone, Drake deserves to be perpetually honored. Even Drake's enemies admired him.

FRANCIS DRAKE — ECHOES OF THE DRAGON'S DRUM

The commander of the Spanish Armada described Drake as a 'great seaman and gifted soldier.'"[92] Though he was a man above men, it is certain that not all raised monuments to him.

Perhaps Drake's contemporaries paint the most accurate historical or biographical portrait. Naturally the people of England, in particular those of Plymouth and the west, mourned the death of Sir Francis Drake as the loss of a great man. Contemporary poets like Charles Fitzgeffrey extolled the virtues of his land's fallen hero in epic style. Explorers who followed his path to the New World often referred to him, and more than one dropped anchor off the coast of Panama where Drake was given back to the sea to pay their respects. Even those in his country who never accepted him as an equal could not deny the role Drake had played in propelling England from a struggling island nation to a leader on the world stage.

Such recognition of a favorite son is to be expected from those who profited from his efforts, but sometimes a person can best be judged by the estimation of his enemies. Those on the high seas held a court of their own kind, and even those Drake plundered realized he dealt much more fairly with others than they had in similar circumstance. More often than not, the Spanish sailors and soldiers he fought against offered him a certain grudging respect. Drake's last opponent Don Alonso de Sotomayor, upon hearing of his death, wrote: "one of the most famous men of his profession that have existed in the world, very courteous and honorable with those who surrendered, of great humanity and gentleness, virtues which must be praised even in an enemy."[93]

But perhaps Drake would have been amused most by the sentiments

FRANCIS DRAKE   ECHOES OF THE DRAGON'S DRUM

of King Philip II. As the king lay ill and hidden away in a monastery, word arrived by way of a servant that his nemesis Francis Drake would antagonize him no more. On hearing this, Spain's king brightened. "It is good news," he said, "and now I will get well."[94] Fewer words could better epitomize the impact England's fallen hero had made on his world. That a wharf rat of no status or family title could so affect the ruler of a great world empire is a testament to the far-reaching influence of Francis Drake.

Drake was both shaped by the Old World into which he was born and the New World he helped explore. Among those influences there can be no doubt that his Christian faith was a significant factor in Drake's life and leadership. His cousin John Hawkins, by all appearances, could take or leave England's Reformation, but not Francis. Foxe's *Book of Martyrs*, printed during Drake's lifetime, often accompanied him on his voyages and reinforced his view of the Roman Catholic Church as predatory. Drake's many voyages and tales of how Conquistadors treated the native population of Mexico and South America did nothing but strengthen his resolve against all things Roman Catholic.

As Dudley writes: "The place of religion—and religious persecution—in Drake's youth must be stressed. At his father's feet, he learned to hate Catholicism as well as the English Catholics who forced the Drakes from their family home and into destitute circumstances. He also learned from his parents to love a Protestant God."[95] Along with Protestantism's view of God came its view of the priesthood of the believers and of God's Word, the Bible. Unlike the Roman Catholic Church, which largely encouraged the ignorance of its adherents, the Reformation that

FRANCIS DRAKE — ECHOES OF THE DRAGON'S DRUM

swept across Europe gave rise to an emphasis on reading the Bible for one's self. The Reformation, therefore, paved the way for the seamen of Plymouth to rise above the state of their birth. Protestant doctrine stressed the individual's comprehension of the Bible. Because of his commitment to this doctrine, Edmund Drake gave his son a gift denied most commoners in Europe—the ability to read and write. Without that, Francis could have never commanded a ship nor earned the respect he found in Elizabeth's court.

This generation's best Drake biographer, John Sugden, considered Julian Corbett to be the greatest of all those who chronicled the life of the Dragon. In his 1898 work, *Drake and the Tudor Navy*, Corbett argues that Sir Francis Drake was a singular factor in making England a significant naval power. Spain imagined itself invincible, and many in England were prone to secretly agree. Henry VIII may have created the modern navy, but "it was Drake who . . . transformed it into a major vehicle of policy. His large-scale expeditions against Spain and the West Indies and his battles in the Channel . . . made it a force in Europe, helped preserve the Reformation and rescued England from invasion."[96] Corbett championed Drake as a strategic and tactical genius whose ideas became the signature of naval power. It was Drake's offensive mindedness, sailing tactics, and line-ahead formations that made the navy of England the power that could stand off the mighty Armada of Spain. Like a Patton or MacArthur of a later era, his brashness often brought him trouble in Elizabeth's court, but his victories and the treasures that accompanied them also earned him the title Sir Francis. As in all generations, success wins most arguments when all is said and done.

Francis Drake — Echoes of the Dragon's Drum

The line between piracy and service to God and country was a very fine one indeed during the early to mid-1500s. Because of Spain's head start in the New World and the pope's edicts that protected his favored nations, England had fewer and fewer places to look to for trade. Sailors, such as those from Plymouth, had little choice but to play the part of a shadow navy for the Queen. This relationship between Queen and privateer brought much needed capital to finance her official military and plausible deniability should things go wrong for her Sea Dogs. It likewise gave them riches beyond measure—as long as they survived.

Drake was born into a system that demanded he play the game of trade and politics the way he did. The rules were set in stone, and the best one could do was chip away around the edges of those rules to forge a place for himself in a society where birth and position meant everything. As much as he respected her, Francis Drake was well aware of how his Queen maneuvered her assets on the international chessboard. One might be in good favor on leaving for the New World only to find things drastically different upon returning. For this reason Drake and his fellow explorers were cautious when they returned home. If things went wrong abroad, Elizabeth's smile might well have turned into a frown. Executions were not uncommon and required little explanation from the Queen. On the other hand, success brought favor and often resulted in the highest possible rank as when Francis was knighted. Even then a Sea Dog was still at the whim of his sovereign and could be demoted in rank or swept clean from the playing board.

It is unfortunate that some in the 21st century judge a man of the 16th century for failing to meet their own standards. As someone observed,

FRANCIS DRAKE   ECHOES OF THE DRAGON'S DRUM

that makes about as much sense as condemning a man for having the wrong skin color. Simon Winchester, writing for the Smithsonian, observed that "historians who take a dim view of empire and war have been busy trying to pull the rug out from under Drake's reputation. Criticizing him for greed and violence, they often judge Drake as though he lived in our times instead of viewing him in proper context: the robustious 16th century."[97] But judging Drake by the standards of his day yields a picture of someone who overcame numerous obstacles to rise above his time. Yes, Drake was driven to make money by waging war at sea, and sometimes he appears lawless to people of a different time; most the military men of the Elizabethan era would be considered mercenaries by modern standards. Naval officers well into the 1800s, were in it—at least in part—for the money. But their pursuit of prize money does not mean that either Sir Francis Drake or Admiral Nelson was incompetent, weak, or unpatriotic. It certainly does not mean they were criminal.

History credits Magellan as the first to circumnavigate the globe, but in truth it was his crew, not their captain, that accomplished that feat. Francis Drake, however, at the helm of his famous *Golden Hind* made that historic trip all the way home to Plymouth. And Drake's exploits and naval career, positioned England to establish colonies in North America by the early 17th century. Spain gained gold and silver that would be spent up in coming wars, but England achieved something more lasting, a land to colonize and through which she could develop her commerce.

Drake was born a commoner in a time when title and name meant

FRANCIS DRAKE   ECHOES OF THE DRAGON'S DRUM

everything. George Washington's ancestors in England were of pedigree and distinction, but not so Francis Drake's. Wade G. Dudley writes that such a lowly birth "did not bode well for his chances at achieving immortality—only dust marks the passage of most such lives."[98] For this reason, Drake became the model of the self-made man for generations to follow.

Nowhere can one better see this picture of Francis Drake as the epitome of individual achievement than upon his return to Plymouth from circumnavigating the world. Hugh Bicheno writes:

> *"Drake went on to become the avatar of the triumph of Protestant English individualism over the termite swarms of Hispano-Popish imperialism, which until relatively recently defined a major element of English national consciousness. He was undoubtedly heroic: bold, fearless and blessed with good fortune. Furthermore, he was born into obscurity and achieved greatness; started dirt poor and died wealthy; consorted with the highest in the land without losing the common touch; and—so important in the English preoccupation with class—he moved in cosmopolitan circles but remained true to his roots."*[99]

That image of Drake's rugged individualism, though diminished, still remains in the collective psyche of the Western World. Therefore it is fitting that when yachtsman, Francis Chichester completed his daring solo trip around the world in 1967, Queen Elizabeth II used Drake's sword to perform the ceremony of knighthood. The poet Greepe summed up Drake's fame in the six lines he penned in 1587:

FRANCIS DRAKE — ECHOES OF THE DRAGON'S DRUM

Ulysses with his navy great
In ten years' time great valour won;
Yet all his time did no such feat
As Drake within one year hath done.
Both Turk and Pope and all our foes
Do dread this Drake wher'er he goes.

To his enemies Sir Francis Drake was El Draco, the Dragon, the incarnation of the Devil. Spanish mothers often warned their children to do their chores and mind their parents or El Draco would come and devour them. But to his admiring countrymen he was a superhero. As John Knox Laughton wrote: "From among all moderns Drake's name stands out as the one that has been associated with almost as many legends as that of Arthur or Charlemagne."[100] If success is the main criteria for legend, then Drake ranks far below others of his day. But the Elizabethan era was one marked by endeavor rather than success. Drake and his fellow Sea Dogs never found the Northwest Passage they searched for; they never established a successful colony in the New Word; and they never opened real trade with the East. However, what Drake did was far greater: he became a legend to believe in, a symbol for the English imagination. He embodied England's announcement that it was an isolated island nation no more.

Some have sought to lessen the scope of Drake's success by claiming he was simply lucky. He didn't set out to circumnavigate the world, but rather knew there was no safe course but to aim the *Golden Hind* away from California. He wasn't exactly following orders when his tactics led to the defeat of the Spanish Armada. Terry

FRANCIS DRAKE   ECHOES OF THE DRAGON'S DRUM

Pratchett wrote; "Scientists have calculated that the chances of something so patently absurd actually existing are millions to one. But magicians have calculated that million-to-one chances crop up nine times out of ten."[101] Fortune, it is said, smiles on those who work the hardest for success. Francis Drake had a knack for accomplishing the million to one, nine times out of ten. There is no doubt that Drake was born at just the right time to accomplish what he did as a commoner. Sugden rightly notes, "the expansion of the Tudor state . . . demanded more talent than high birth could supply."[102] Honest biographers are quick to acknowledge that even when Drake was lucky, he made more out of that fortune than most ever dreamed possible. There was much more to this man from Plymouth than good fortune. Francis Drake had a natural skill for sea warfare and a sense of leadership. Unlike most sailors, he was also an intelligent, persuasive orator, which gave him the tools he needed to gain support in circles far above his station of birth. These traits and more made him an able businessman, magistrate, and parliamentarian.

Legends often give birth to legends—sometimes to legends that become something bigger than the men who bred them. One such legend concerns Francis Drake's drum. In Buckland Abbey there hangs a walnut barreled snare drum that surely belonged to Drake's time. Legend says this drum accompanied Drake as he sailed the *Golden Hind* around the world. Legend also says that Englishmen, in dire and hopeless times, have heard that drumbeat calling them to persevere.

In 1897, Henry Newbolt echoed the legend with these words:

FRANCIS DRAKE — ECHOES OF THE DRAGON'S DRUM

DRAKE he's in his hammock an' a thousand mile away,
(Capten, art tha sleepin' there below?)
Slung atween the round shot in Nombre Dios Bay,
An' dreamin' arl the time o' Plymouth Hoe.
Yarnder lumes the island, yarnder lie the ships,
Wi' sailor lads a-dancin' heel-an'-toe,
An' the shore-lights flashin', an' the night-tide dashin'
He sees et arl so plainly as he saw et long ago.

Drake he was a Devon man, an' ruled the Devon seas,
(Capten, art tha sleepin' there below?),
Rovin' tho' his death fell, he went wi' heart at ease,
An' dreamin' arl the time o' Plymouth Hoe,
"Take my drum to England, hang et by the shore,
Strike et when your powder's runnin' low;
If the Dons sight Devon, I'll quit the port o' Heaven,
An' drum them up the Channel as we drummed them long ago."

Drake he's in his hammock till the great Armadas come,
(Capten, art tha sleepin' there below?),
Slung atween the round shot, listenin' for the drum,
An' dreamin' arl the time o' Plymouth Hoe.
Call him on the deep sea, call him up the Sound,
Call him when ye sail to meet the foe;
Where the old trade's plyin' an' the old flag flyin',
They shall find him, ware an' wakin', as they found him long ago.

FRANCIS DRAKE — ECHOES OF THE DRAGON'S DRUM

The legend of Drake's drum reappeared during World War II. In August 1940, during the darkness of the Battle of Britain, the BBC went on air with a program entitled, "Drake's Drum." That same September, as the RAF turned back the Luftwaffe from the daytime skies of London, two army officers swore they heard the drum again on the Hampshire shore. Often during those uncertain years of the War, the people of England were reminded of Drake's words, "There must be a beginning of any great matter, but the continuing unto the end until it be thoroughly finished yields the true glory."[103] Those words gave way to a prayer repeated a thousand times over across the British Isles:

Picture of a replica of Drake's Drum, from the Buckland Abbey education centre.

> *O Lord God, when thou givest to thy servants to endeavour any great matter, grant us also to know that it is not the beginning, but the continuing of the same unto the end, until it be thoroughly finished, which yieldeth the true glory.*

In every crisis, whenever his country struggles, Drake has been there. From Nelson to Churchill to Thatcher the spirit of the man who rose from nothing to attempt the impossible doggedly beats across the sea. Perhaps even now some schoolboy accosted by a bully twice his size, some solider on a distant battle field, or some mother unsure of the next day for her child hears a sound wafting across the waters of the Channel. Perhaps they hear echoes—echoes of the Dragon's drum.

JOHN STOW, THE LIFE AND DEATH OF SIR FRANCIS DRAKE (1615)

He was more skilfull in all poyntes of Navigation than any that ever was before his time, in his time, or since his death. He was also of a perfect memory, great Observation, Eloquent by Nature, Skilfull in Artillery, expert and apt to let blood, and give Physicke unto his people according to the Climats. He was Low of stature, of strong limbs, broade Breasted, round headed, brown hayre, full Bearded, his eyes round, Large and cleare, well favoured, fayre, and of a cheerefull countenance.

His name was a terrour to the French, Spaniard, Portugal, and Indians. Many Princes of Italy, Germany and others, as well enemies as friends in his lifetime desired his Picture. He was the second that ever went through the straights of Magellan, and the first that ever went round about the world. He was married unto two wives, both young, yet he himselfe and ten of his brethren dyed without Issue. He made his youngest brother Thomas his heir who was with him in most and chiefest of his Imployments. In briefe, he was as famous in Europe and America as Tamberlaine in Asia and Africa.

In his imperfections hee was Ambitious for honour.

Unconstant in amity

Greatly affected to Popularity.[104]

ACADEMIE ROYALE des SCIENCES
et quelques autres et sur les memoires les plus recens
PAR M. DE L'ISLE
GROENLAND
CANADA
GOLFE DE MEXIQUE
Detroit de Magellan
Antarctique
MER GLACIALE
TERRES
DU NORD

Notes

1) William Manchester, *The Last Lion: Winston Spencer Churchill Alone* (New York: Delta, 1989), i.

2) Charles N. Wheeler, "Fight to Disarm His Life's Work, Henry Ford Vows," *Chicago Tribune*, May 25, 1916.

3) Oliver Seeler, "Francis Drake in Nova Albion: The Mystery Restored." Drake.mcn.org http://drake.mcn.org/script.htm. Accessed 09/10/2013.

4) Victor Hugo, *Works: Ninety-Three*, 188.

5) N.A.M. Rodger, "The Pirate King," *The New York Times* http://www.nytimes.com/books/98/10/25/reviews/981025.25rodgert.html. October 25, 1998.

6) Ibid.

7) William Wood, *Elizabethan Sea-Dogs: A Chronicle of Drake and His Companions* (Yale University Press, 1918), Kindle Edition, 148-153.

8) Wade G. Dudley, *Drake: For God, Queen, and Plunder* (Washington: Potomoc Books, Inc., 2003), Kindle Edition, 156-165.

9) Elaine W. Fowler, *English Sea Power in the Early Tudor Period (1485-1558)* (Ithaca, New York: Cornell University Press, 1965), 7-8.

10) Yale Law School, Lillian Goldman Law Library. "The Letters Patents of King Henry the Seventh Granted unto Iohn Cabot and his Three Sonnes, Lewis, Sebastion and Sancius for the Discouerie of New and Unknowen Lands." www.avalon.law.yale.edu/15th_century/cabot01.asp. Accessed 09/09/2013.

11) Wood, 180.

12) Ibid, 214-215.

13) John Sugden, *Sir Francis Drake* (London: Random House, 2006), Kindle Edition, location 80-83.

14) Wood, 1933.

15) Ibid, 733.

16) Ibid, 392-399.

17) Hugh Bicheno, *Elizabeth's Sea Dogs* (London: Conway Publishing, 2010), Kindle Edition, location111-117.

18) Maggie Secara, editor. Elizabethan Sumptuary Statutes "Who Wears What I." www.Elizabethan.org. www.elizabethan.org/sumptuary/who-wears-what.html. Accessed 09/09/2013

19) Stephen Alford, *The Watchers* (New York: Bloomsbury Publishing Plc., 2012), Kindle Edition, location 118-141.

20) Fowler, 38-39.

21) Wood, 76.

22) Eric Metaxas, *Amazing Grace* (HarperCollins, 2006), Kindle Edition, location 100.

23) Sudgen, 778-787.

24) Ernle Bradford, *The Wind Commands Me*, (New York: Harcort, Brace & World, Inc., 1965), 7-8.

25) Wood, 733.

26) Ibid.

27) Angus Konstam, *Pirates* (Guilford, CN: Lyons Press, 2008), Kindle Edition, location 37.

28) Fowler, 18.

29) Baron Walter Runciman, *Drake, Nelson, and Napoleon* (New York: G.P. Putnam and Sons, 1920), p. 20.

30) *Report on the Discovery of Peru*, (New York: Burt Franklin, publisher), p. 54.

31) Bradford, 33.

32) Sugden, 1098-1114.

33) Wood, 105-106.

34) Ibid, 104-107.

35) Sugden, 1923-1936.

36) Ibid, 2230-2238.

37) Ibid, 2255.

38) Ibid, 2404-2407.

39) Bicheno, 78-96.

40) Samuel Bawlf, *The Secret Voyage of Sir Francis Drake* (New York: Bloomsbury Publishing Plc., 2003), Kindle Edition, location 846-849.

41) Ibid, 872-873.

42) Ibid, 112-116.

43) Ibid.

44) Harry Kelsey, *Sir Francis Drake: The Queen's Pirate* (Yale University Press, 2000), 83.

45) Bawlf, 1023-1029.

46) Ibid, 1045-1047.

47) Ibid, 1117-1120.

48) Internet Archive. Cornell University Library, "Select Naval Documents (1922)" www.archives.org. http://www.archive.org/stream/cu31924028018020/cu31924028018020_djvi/txt. Accessed 09/09/2013.

49) Bawlf, 1344-1350.

50) Ibid, 1358.

51) Ibid, 1362.

FRANCIS DRAKE — ECHOES OF THE DRAGON'S DRUM

52) Ibid, 1401-1417.

53) Sugden, 2926-2931.

54) Ibid, 2892.

55) Ibid, 2906.

56) Bawlf, 1513.

57) Ibid, 1561.

58) Ibid, 1768-1783.

59) Ibid, 1717-1721.

60) Internet Archive. The Hakluyt Society, "The World Encompassed by Sir Francis Drake," www.archive.org, http://archive.org/stream/worldencompassed16drak/worldencompassed16drak_djvu.txt. Accessed 09/09/2013.

61) Bawlf, 2391.

62) Wood, 1086-1088.

63) Dudley, 674-681.

64) Charles River Editors, *British Legends: The Life and Legacy of Sir Francis Drake* (Charles River Editors, 2007), Kindle Edition, location 474-511.

65) Ibid, 517.

66) Bawlf, 2628-2660.

67) Ibid.

68) Dudley, 437.

69) Sugden, 4230-4241.

70) Ibid, 4234-4357.

FRANCIS DRAKE ECHOES OF THE DRAGON'S DRUM

71) Dudley, 731.

72) Ibid.

73) Angus Konstam, *The Great Expedition: Sir Francis Drake on the Spanish Main* (Cambridge: Osprey Publishing, 2011), Kindle Edition, location 55-64.

74) Ibid, 527-529.

75) Ibid, 640.

76) Ibid, 859-861.

77) Dudley, 817.

78) Ibid.

79) Konstam, 1279.

80) Ibid, 1290-1303.

81) Sugden, 5670-5686.

82) Dudley, 847-848.

83) Ibid, 919-921.

84) Sugden, 6448-6451.

85) Dudley, 1021-1027.

86) Ibid, 1131-1136.

87) Sugden, 8283-8290.

88) Bicheno, 4081-4089.

89) Sugden, 8592-8595.

90) Ibid, 8673-8676.

91) Charles River Editors, 770-783

92) The Drake Exploration Society. "Drake the Man." www.indrakeswake.co.uk http://wwwindrakeswake.co.uk/Society/drake.htm. Accessed 09/10/2013.

93) Sugden, 8760-8763.

94) Ibid, 8607.

95) Dudley, 1198-1201.

96) Sugden, 8853-8858.

97) Simon Winchester, "Sir Francis Drake is Still Capable of Kicking Up a Fuss." www.smithsonian.com http://www.smithsonianmag.com/history-archaeology/drake-abstract.html. Accessed 09/10/2013.

98) Dudley, 1193-1194.

99) Bicheno, 1589-1594.

100) John Knox Laughton, *Dictionary of National Biography, 1885-1900, Vol. 15*, p. 441.

101) Terry Pratchett, *Mort: The Fourth Discworld Novel,* HarperCollins: New York, 1987.

102) Sugden, 120-128.

103) Ibid, 8807.

104) The Drake Exploration Society. http://www.indrakeswake.co.uk/Drake/realdrake.htm

BIBLIOGRAPHY

Alford, Stephen. *The Watchers*. New York: Bloomsbury Publishing Plc., 2012. Kindle Edition.

Bawlf, Samuel. *The Secret Voyage of Sir Francis Drake*. New York: Bloomsbury Publishing Plc., 2003. Kindle Edition.

Bradford, Ernle. *The Wind Commands Me*. New York: Harcort, Brace & World, Inc., 1965.

Bicheno, Hugh. *Elizabeth's Sea Dogs*. London: Conway Publishing, 2010. Kindle Edition.

Bradford, Ernle. *The Wind* Commands Me. Harcourt Brace & World, 2006.

Charles Rivers Editors. *British Legends: The Life and Legacy of Sir Francis Drake*. Charles River Editors, 2007. Kindle Edition.

Cooper, John. *The Queen's Agent*. New York and London: Pegasus Books, 2013. Kindle Edition.

Corbett, Julian S. *The Successors of Drake*. New York: Burt Franklin, 1900.

Dictionary of National Biography, 1885-1900, Vol. 15.

Drake Exploration Society. www.indrakeswake.co.uk.

Dudley, Wade G. *Drake: For God, Queen, and Plunder*. Washington: Potomoc Books, Inc. 2003.

Fowler, Elaine W. *English Sea Power in the Early Tudor Period (1485-1558)*. Ithaca, New York: Cornell University Press, 1965.

Hugo, Victor. *Works: Ninety-Three*. New York: The Century Company. 1905.

Internet Archive. www.archives.org.

Kelsey, Harry. *Sir Francis Drake: The Queen`s Pirate*. Yale University Press. 2000.

Konstam, Angus. *Pirates*. Guilford, CN: Lyons Press, 2008. Kindle Edition.

Konstam, Angus. The Great Expedition: Sir Francis Drake on the Spanish Main. Cambridge: Osprey Publishing, 2011. Kindle Edition.

Manchester, William. *The Last Lion: Winston Spencer Churchill Alone*. New York: Delta. 1989.

Metaxas Eric. *Amazing Grace*. New York: HarperCollins. 2006.

Report on the Discovery of Peru. New York: Burt Franklin.

Rodger, N.A.M., "The Pirate King." *New York Times*, October 25, 1998.

Runciman, Baron Walter. *Drake, Nelson, and Napoleon*. New York: G.P. Putnam and Sons. 1920.

Secara, Maggie. Elizabethan Sumptuary Statutes, www.elizabethan.org.

Seeler, Oliver. "Francis Drake in Nova Albion: The Mystery Restored." Nova Albion Research.1996-1997, www.drake.mcn.org/script.htm.

Sugden, John. *Sir Francis Drake*. London: Random House. 2006. Kindle Edition

Wheeler, Charles N. "Fight to Disarm His Life's Work, Henry Ford Vows." *Chicago Tribune*, May 25, 1916.

Winchester, Simon. "Sir Francis Drake is Still Capable of Kicking Up a Fuss." *Smithsonian Magazine*. www.smithsonianmag.com.

Wood, William. *Elizabethan Sea-Dogs: A Chronicle of Drake and His Companions*. Yale University Press. 1918. Kindle Edition.

Yale Law School, Lillian Goldman Law Library. "The Letters Patents of King Henry the Seventh Granted unto Iohn Cabot and his Three Sonnes, Lewis, Sebastion and Sancius for the Discouerie of New and Unknowen Lands." www.avalon.law.yale.edu.